# ASWB Clinical Study Guide 2020-2021

## Social Work Exam Prep with 450 Questions and Detailed Answer Explanations (New Outline and 3 Full Practice Tests)

# Table of Contents

# Chapter 1: ASWB Clinical Exam

## About the Exam

The Association of Social Work Boards (ASWB) clinical examination is one of the steps in the licensing process. The ASWB clinical examination is used in the United States and its territories, as well as in the Canadian Provinces of Manitoba, Alberta, and British Columbia. Some professions must have a license; the field of social work is no exception.

Social workers are required to take and pass the ASWB clinical examination to earn their license. Those who pass the exam are generally qualified for state licensure for social work practice. The following are the five categories offered by ASWB for their social work licensure examination:

- Associate
- Bachelors
- Masters
- Advanced Generalists
- Clinical

ASWB levels are unique, and the requirement for each level may vary from state to state as some areas or states may not offer all five categories of exams. The exams assess the candidate's skills, knowledge, and abilities in four main content areas being human development, assessment, ethics, and psychotherapy. Each level covers similar topics, but the extent of the detail varies as the candidates move towards higher levels.

## Test Format

Candidates with a minimum of a Master's Degree in Social Work and two years of clinical work experience after obtaining their degree are eligible to sit for the Clinical exam. The test format is a computer-delivered examination that consists of 170 MCQs (multiple-choice questions).

Candidates have four hours to complete all four categories of practice. Each question has four options, with only one correct answer. Only 150 out of 170 will be scored. The remaining 20 questions are included to evaluate the validity of the question for future exams.

The test consists of different content areas, divided as follows:

- Human development, behavior, and diversity in the society/environment – 24%
- Assessment, treatment planning and diagnosis – 30%
- Professional ethics and values – 19%

- Psychotherapy, case management and clinical interventions – 27%

Knowledge, skills, and abilities (KSAs) examined in these content areas include human behavior and growth in social environments, discrimination, professional development, issues related to ethics and professional values, management of cases, therapeutic relationship, assessment and diagnosis, planning, biopsychosocial collateral date, history, and treatment.

## Exam Development

ASWB structures its content outline very accurately and carefully, as it observes the result of significant surveys conducted for thousands of practicing social workers. It helps them to establish relevant categories of the exams offered with content that will be measured on the exams has culminated from the content outline for each examination. These content outlines serve as the blueprints for the exam and also for generating passing scores.

A candidate taking the ASWB examination needs to answer an estimate of 93 to 107 questions correctly out of 150 to earn a passing score. You are not scored based on attempting all questions, but solely on those you answered correctly. However, the actual number of correct answers required depends on the difficulty and the version of the exam you take.

ASWB's Examination Committee reviews every question in the examination, whereas the group who writes the questions are practicing social workers who reflect diversity in geography, ethnicity, practice setting, and race. Experienced social workers approve all the questions before they appear in the exam. Each category in the exam has its bank of questions.

## Tips and Tricks for Best Performance

Preparing for an ASWB clinical exam can be overwhelming as it covers such diverse content. In categorizing the exam over the different content areas focusing on the various topics. Each of these divisions helps in assessing the candidates, developing a competent exam, and in the scoring. The four areas that the exam will cover consist of the following topics:

Human Development and Diversity and Behavior in the Environment category includes interpersonal relationships, theories of sexual, spiritual, and human development throughout one's life, effects of abuse, stress, and trauma, conflict theories, and gender identity concepts.

Psychotherapy, Clinical Interventions, and Case Management category includes verbal and non-verbal communication, anger and stress management, networking methods, building and maintaining relationships, and family therapy.

The Assessment, Diagnosis, and Treatment Planning category includes psychosocial stress, the impact of immigration, behavioral dysfunction, methods of risk assessment, and active listening.

The Professional Values and Ethics category includes confidentiality, safe and positive work environment, evidence-based practice, informed consent, and professional values and principles.

## Sample Question:

| | |
|---|---|
| Exam Category: | Clinical |
| Content Area: | I. Human Development, Diversity, and Behavior in the Environment |
| Competency: | IB. Social injustice and Discrimination |
| KSA: | Role of social workers to support minorities against social injustice |
| Question: | Which approach is used by social workers to help and support the minorities and the most vulnerable groups against social injustice?<br><br>(A) Policy advocacy<br>(B) Norms and values<br>(C) Coercion policies<br>(D) Support groups |

Key:          A

10/5/20

# Chapter 2: Introduction to Social Work

## What is social work?

Social work is a profession focusing on providing help to people in need. It includes providing services, building communities with psychotherapy and counseling, developing health and education services, and helping in the formation of social policies.

It is a practice-based profession but has recently emerged as a separate academic discipline. It promotes development and change, social collaborations, and the empowerment of oppressed or repressed members of society.

Social workers approach every problem from many different perspectives, which may include social, individual, psychological, or political angles. Their work encompasses a variety of roles, such as counseling, advocacy, political activism, or group works. There are several diverse specializations within the discipline, which can be divided into three categories, namely:

### 1. Family, children, and school-oriented social workers

This category consists of people who help children, families, and are engaged with the schooling systems to resolve problems. For example, social workers may help with the placement of orphaned children into foster homes, and work with teachers or students to address issues like learning disabilities, bullying, and other problems children may face in school.

Social workers help in connecting struggling parents with jobs and better resources to enable them to provide improved care for their children. The Bureau of Labor Statistics states that family, children, and school social workers are the most common, globally.

### 2. Public health and medical social workers

The second most common category of social workers is within the healthcare system, with a rapidly growing demand for public health workers. These social workers are committed to helping the sick and those with chronic medical conditions to find adequate care. They often help in getting health insurance and financial coverage for those who cannot afford their treatments and can assist in locating services like in-home nursing care.

Some in this field are trained to provide counseling to those suffering from a terminal illness. They also play a significant role in raising awareness regarding health problems that are neglected and offer the best solutions.

### 3. Mental health and substance abuse social workers

This category of social workers focus on resolving mental health problems or drug addiction issues. They are skilled in providing specially tailored interventions for those in need by assisting in finding rehabilitative programs or offering counseling sessions. A significant part of their role is participating in outreach and preventative programs to raise awareness amongst people to avoid exacerbating these problems in society. Mental health and substance abuse are growing specializations within the field of social work.

## Where do social workers work?

There is a wide range of employment settings for social workers. Their specialization determines this and in what capacity. For example, childcare social workers may often have to move around from case to case, or some may be employed at a school or foster home service. On the contrary, healthcare social workers are usually more fixed in their roles and employment.

Most social workers work in an office space; however, they may have to travel offsite to visit clients or attend meetings at times. The more traditional institutions employing social workers include schools, hospitals, prisons, mental health clinics, senior citizen centers, public social agencies, or military barracks. Other licensed social workers choose to set up in private practice, working independently to help and provide their services to clients. As previously stated, the demand for social workers is increasing as new issues emerge in our society daily.

## History of Social Work

The history of social work dates back to the Middle-Ages when church-based ministering to the less fortunate evolved into the social justice and the philanthropic movements of the 19th century. Today, social work is still deeply rooted within these originating beliefs, which include community equality, compassion, and equity for all.

The social work profession that we know today has roots belonging to three distinct entities—the poverty relief social policies, as created by the English Poor Laws during the 17th century. The casework method, as developed by the British Charity Organization Society (CSO) in the mid-19th century. The idea of socio-political actions focused on addressing social injustices originating from the settlement house movement.

The primary foundation of the field emerges from a moral obligation to provide help to the vulnerable segments of society. Social work is intrinsically linked to charity work, as most religions preach that every individual must aid those less privileged. For example, the Christian church, with its significant influence in Europe during the Middle-Ages, made charity a social obligation for all, considering this a sign of virtue and devotedness to the religion.

As societies progressed in a time of significant industrialization and urbanization, the work formally conducted by religious establishments, was formalized into social welfare services.

While the industrial revolution made great leaps in scientific and technological developments, causing more people to flock towards cities throughout the Western world. As this happened, more social problems appeared, requiring greater social activism. During the 18th century, new methods for giving aid emerged to address these social issues creating several rescue societies to help resolve problems relating to poverty, disease, mental illness, and prostitution.

The American Civil War was a significant event that resulted in the banning of slavery in the United States. This historical event increased the reality of how prevalent social inequality was and the need to address it. After the war, many measures were taken to rebuild the country, including helping displaced families after freeing millions of slaves, who required necessities like food, clothing, and housing. The US government launched a social services program to provide aid to these people.

In response to social injustice, such events lead to significant reforms during the 19th century. Many efforts were made to raise awareness concerning mental illness, child labor in sweatshops and factories, and the condition of poverty-stricken countries.

Schools for social work started emerging, but because it was still not considered a separate profession, due to it lacking the application of theoretical knowledge to practical problems. A movement to certify the profession was started, boosting formal learning opportunities within this field.

The professionalization of social work started by focusing on casework and scientific methods to resolve societal issues. They were launching university programs regarding social work to incorporate more scientific methods into the field. These workers were committed to helping others to attain justice and equality of rights.

The formation of the National Association of Social Workers (NASW) in 1955 was a massive step in promoting the field of social work. It incorporated the learning of advanced social policies, professional development, and formal educational opportunities, starting the acceptance of social work as a separate profession around the world. Since then, in both the 20th and 21st centuries, social workers have become the champions of those needing assistance. It coincides with the increased number of movements for social reforms.

Today, social workers lead the way towards justice and equity for all through public and private charitable organizations that serve communities and individuals in need. It is one of the most diverse fields and has a range of opportunities which is helping the profession grow significantly faster than other occupations.

## Social Work Pioneers

While discussing the history of social work, it is essential to mention the notable people who founded and were pioneers in this field. The first medical social workers, known as hospital almoners, worked in medical facilities. Mary Stewart was the first lady almoner in Britain in 1985.

A young student named Jane Addams founded the US Settlement House Movement to create settlement houses in poor cities for middle-class social workers to alleviate poverty in the region. Because of this movement, 413 settlements across 32 states were established and assisted in improving the lives of the poor.

Other notable social workers include Frances Perkins, who served as Franklin D. Roosevelt's secretary of labor and was instrumental in the drafting of the new legislation in 1940. Whitney M. Young. Jr. was one of the earliest trailblazers who later became the president of the NASW and was a crucial figure in the civil rights movement. Dorothy Height, Jeanette Rankin, Harry Hopkins, and Edward Thomas Divine are all also notable names within the field of social work.

## The Six Values of Social Work

According to the US Bureau of Labor Statistics, the number of social workers is expected to increase by more than 100,000 by 2026. Regardless of their employment setting, each social worker has taken an oath to adhere to the professional code of ethics by the National Association of Social Workers. This code of ethics first came to existence in 1996 and was revised in 2017.

The NASW code of ethics is a guide on how social workers should conduct themselves. It outlines six ethical principles or core values that all social workers should achieve and apply in their professional lives. These six core values comprise of:

(1) Service

(2) Social justice

(3) Dignity

(4) Human relationships

10/5/20

(5) Integrity

(6) Competence

## 1- Service

The primary goal of social workers is to help others and address social ills present in society, making service a significant value for all social workers, as all other core values stem from this.

Social workers prioritize the needs of others before their interests, using their knowledge and skills for the sole purpose of helping others. In addition to paid services, they volunteer their time without financial compensation. They are determined to provide help, resources, and other benefits that can help the people in their society to reach their maximum potential and to live life comfortably. They use their abilities to help their clients through social problems such as child abuse, residential instability, or drug dependency.

## 2- Social Justice

The second core value in the code of ethics is social justice. Social workers involve themselves in political matters by advocating on behalf of the vulnerable and oppressed segments of the society who are unable to do so themselves, bringing issues such as poverty, discrimination, homelessness, and pay inequality to the forefront. They are committed to create awareness about fundamental rights and educate people regarding equality. They also raise their voices to promote public sensitivity towards injustice in society and encourage people to take action by embracing diversity and respecting all cultures. Social workers promote equal opportunities for all narrative amongst their clients.

## 3- Dignity

Every individual is unique and has different cultural and social values. Being mindful of these differences is a crucial aspect of being a social worker as they need to understand these differences and treat everyone with respect. The dignity of every human being should be maintained regardless of their background or values, and the social worker's role is to promote their client's abilities and opportunities to help them improve their situations.

Social workers must understand that their duties are towards individuals from every walk of life and hence the society as a whole. They need to think of the collective interest of the community and pay no heed to the differences between people.

## 4- Human Relationships

Another core value of social work is to recognize the significance of human relationships and how they form the foundation of society. Facilitating these relationships creates positive change helping to develop affiliations amongst people, which is an essential vehicle for advocacy and equity. It builds up societal cooperation and harmony with social workers engaging potential partners who can work together to create, maintain, or improve the well-being of families, towns, and whole communities. Social workers must be skilled in maintaining positive and meaningful relationships amongst individuals through excellent communication and patience.

## 5- Integrity

Since social workers need to facilitate good relationships and work for the improvement of people's lives, they must be trustworthy. Each worker should be aware of their profession's goals, values, and principles. They must maintain the standards of the profession and uphold them regardless of their circumstances. They need to have integrity so that their clients feel at ease with them and can rely on them. Exhibiting honesty, responsibility, and compassion is necessary for all social workers allowing them to promote their organizations and create the most value for the communities that they serve.

## 6- Competence

Social workers are required to have undergraduate or postgraduate degrees in their respective fields. However, most workers learn the most through their work experience. NASW's code of ethics has emphasized that each social worker must practice their profession with competence, never misrepresenting their skills or knowledge to their clients. Moreover, to remain competent, every social worker must continue to expand their knowledge and skills to contribute more to society and make meaningful contributions to the field.

The significance of values and ethics in social work is much more than complying with a set of rules and regulations. Instead, it requires workers to be passionate about improving the lives of the vulnerable and oppressed.

# Different Levels of Social Work

Social work can be considered to have an interdisciplinary nature due to the complex contexts and diverse settings in which social workers are often required to work, being why the field is said to operate on different levels. There are three different levels of social work practice that exist today. These are the micro-level, the mezzo level, and the macro-level of social work. It is essential to understand that while these levels are referred to as being different from each other, they are often co-occurring. Each level has some influence on the other.

## The Micro Level of Social Work

The most common type of social work practice occurs at the micro-level. At this level, social workers interact with individuals and families to help them resolve personal and interpersonal issues. It involves the direct interaction of social workers with their clients and includes day-to-day activities.

Some common examples of social work at the micro-level include counseling centers, social service agencies, and hospitals. In these employment settings, social workers perform a range of duties, including finding adequate housing facilities for the homeless or providing individual counseling services to disturbed individuals. Services such as family therapy, trauma work, refugee management, or drug abuse rehabilitation also fall under the umbrella of micro social work.

## The Mezzo Level of Social Work

Mezzo level of social work takes place at a broader scale to include groups instead of just focusing on individuals. These groups consist of families, businesses, schools, local organizations, neighborhoods, and communities. Mezzo level social work is focused on addressing issues on a larger scale. They ensure that the needs of these small groups are being understood and treated with respect. Therefore, it is valuable in creating small-scale, social, and institutional changes. Mezzo social workers are not limited to this level as they also engaged in macro or micro social work.

Some examples of social work within the mezzo level is support and advocacy work within refugee communities, creating educational campaigns, and working to develop sustainable neighborhoods.

## The Macro Level of Social Work

The macro-level of social work is associated with broad and high-level societal systems. It affects entire communities, cities, and even countries. It involves helping clients by intervening in systems that are beyond the reach of the ordinary people.

Macro social workers are engaged in petitioning for funds by involving the government authorities, or being involved in drafting legislative laws for countries, and the organizing of nation-wide activist campaigns.

## Working Across the Levels

Some social workers specialize in one level of the field, while the majority are involved in all three levels in one way or another. Thus, it is crucial to understand how each level works individually, as well as how they interact with each other.

For example, if a school counselor is working to help a child who is facing some difficulties at school and is acting out, he is involved at the micro-level of social work. As the counselor finds that the child is exposed to some negative situations at home, he would then move to the mezzo level getting involved in household matters that affect the child negatively. He would try to address the problems in the child's relationships.

This social worker is now is working simultaneously on both levels, but should this can move to include the macro-level of social work. For example, if he discovers that the problems in the family are due to financial instability, he could then move towards advocating for better job training and unemployment benefits within this community.

With this example, it is clear why all social workers must understand every level of social work so that they can understand the situation from multiple perspectives. Being a successful social worker is dependent on the ability to navigate and combine all three levels seamlessly. It delivers the best outcomes for clients, their families, their communities, and, eventually, entire societies.

10/5/20

# Chapter 3: Service

## Explaining Service

The definition of service is "the action of helping or doing work for someone." It is the foundation on which the field of social work is based. Social work is a profession based purely on providing services to help people in need with the duties consisting of them drawing on their knowledge, experience, skills, and values to help address social issues and those affected by them. Therefore, to be a social worker, you must have a passion for making a difference in people's lives in some capacity.

The value of "service" has the underlying ethical principle of the need and desire to help the vulnerable and to contribute towards addressing social problems. They must elevate providing services to others above their own needs, requiring ample motivation as the profession not only entails a simple office job, but it is much more.

Service towards others can take many forms. Whether you specialize in a particular area of social work or try to engage in different fields simultaneously, being a social worker, requires you to put in the time and effort to resolve social issues. Social workers are often involved in volunteer work with their primary motivation being to improve the lives of their clients, who are usually not able to afford to pay for their services. Hence, social workers who volunteer their time will provide their services for free to such clients.

Social workers are required to work on behalf of clients who cannot do so themselves. Responsible steps to ensure the interests of clients are met and their rights safeguarded must be taken. The Code of Ethics of the National Association of Social Workers has some essential guidelines that must be followed by all social workers.

### Guidelines Regarding Services

Social workers should make reasonable efforts to ensure the continuity of their services and providing their customers with adequate support. Should they be unable to work due to the unavailability of electronic communication, contraction of illness, relocation, or an accident. In such circumstances, they should refer the client to a colleague or inform their organization so that steps can be taken to address the issue.

Social workers are required to act responsibly and refer clients to other professionals who could provide a better service or expertise to resolve the client's problem. In this regard, they should not hesitate or act selfishly. Fulfilling the client's needs should be their priority, no matter who helps them, and facilitating an orderly transfer of responsibility is a necessity. It is important to note that personal gains or any payments made for such references would be considered unethical.

Another essential guideline for social workers is knowing when to terminate their services. They must immediately terminate providing services to clients when they are no longer serving their needs or interests. It is not wise to waste time or resources by prolonging a professional relationship when it is not serving any purpose.

On the contrary, if the client's needs are not met, services should not be terminated abruptly, and all factors must be taken into consideration before such a step is taken. Social workers must take responsible measures to avoid abandoning their clients in their time of need and minimize any adverse effects it may cause.

Moreover, social workers are not allowed to discontinue their services in case of any social, financial, or romantic interest with the client, which is considered very unprofessional and unethical. It is crucial for social workers to notify their clients before discontinuing their services, and should ease the client's process by facilitating their transfer of services and helping them cope with the change.

## The Concepts of Altruism and Selflessness

The concept of altruism is fundamental to the core values of social work and has an interesting history. The word originated from Latin and coined by Auguste Comte, a French philosopher in the 19th century. He used the term to describe the ethical doctrine in which people had a moral obligation to devote themselves to the service of others. It included renouncing any self-interest; therefore, selflessness and altruism go hand in hand.

There are many philosophical examples based on the nature of altruism. These are seen in the teachings of major religions in the world today, where people are motivated to be compassionate towards others to achieve internal happiness, for example, in Buddhism.

### What is Altruism?

The meaning of altruism is to act to promote the welfare of others even if it results in a disadvantage for yourself. It refers to the motive for the behaviors of individuals that are primarily focused on helping others in relieving their distress. An altruist is motivated by the concern for and well-being of others, and is intrinsically in a person's nature. They do not demand anything in return or expect gratitude, recognition, or repayment for their help or service.

Human beings are believed to be fundamentally selfish creatures; however, evidence states that the first impulse of people is to cooperate rather than compete with others.

According to evolutionary scientists, human beings have very deep-rooted altruistic traits because cooperation and help amongst each other ensures the species survival. Thus, altruism can be considered an essential part of social instincts.

As previously discussed, social work means helping individuals and communities in need and working towards making their lives better. The motivation behind social work is based on the concepts of altruism and selflessness. People who choose social work as a profession are more likely to have strong humanitarian values. They feel a sense of responsibility towards other members of the community and believe in giving back. They are more empathetic and compassionate towards others, which could be due to the environment they were raised in, or just a natural intrinsic trait. Social workers tend to have more altruistic motives and apply these practices in many different contexts.

A variety of other factors can influence altruistic behavior. For example, the relationship between the social worker and the client is significant. Empathy is also affiliated with altruistic helping or social work as it requires people to take into account the perspective of the person in need and being empathetic towards their situation, fostering compassionate caring.

It requires social workers to identify with the person needing help as this connection facilitates a better process. The awareness of the needs of others, combined with the desire to fulfill them, is classified as altruism. We can thus infer that altruism is synonymous with selflessness, and both provide the primary motivation for social workers to engage in their work.

## The Importance of Altruism

Altruism is studied in many fields, such as psychology, economics, biology, and sociology. In sociology, it is explicitly used to learn why some individuals in particular societies endanger their lives or risk their well-being for the benefit of others. These include people who spend their time, resources, and knowledge to provide services to people outside their families and close friends. It describes the role of a social worker and its importance in the formation of a good society.

A direct link can be established between altruism, selflessness, and building a good society or in a broader sense, it corresponds to social solidarity. It consists of activities that are intended to raise the welfare of others, which encompass the micro to macro continuum, as they include services relating to individuals, groups, organizations, and the whole world. These services require generosity, virtue, philanthropy, communal cooperation, and universal solidarity.

Similarly, the subject of morality includes making distinctions between good and evil and right and wrong. These distinctions are a vital aspect of each individual's thoughts, judgments, and inevitably their actions. They exist in all cultural systems around the world, providing meaning for each culture and giving a sense of what is desirable and what is not.

For example, intergroup relations and individual aspects are norms in these cultural systems. Therefore, altruism and social solidarity are also related to morality. Altruism and selflessness have intrinsic scientific and public policy relevance in the creation of excellent and well-functioning societies.

Thus, altruism is an essential component of social welfare, the ultimate goal of social work. Incorporating this value into individual lives can lead to the formation of thriving communities that can take responsibility for every member of their society. Without the existence of altruism, communities would not prosper together, and it would result in social problems and injustices. Moreover, the lack of altruistic activities towards better communities can also lead to selfish societies that spiral into disaster.

# Chapter 4: Dignity and Worth

The dignity and worth of an individual are cornerstones in a social worker's vision. First and foremost, these values help them treat each individual with care and ultimate regard and aid in formulating ethical principals

Dignity is a fundamental concept in theologies, moral, and political philosophies all over the world. It manifests itself as an essential theme in national and international constitutions. To treat everyone with dignity, social workers need to learn to be mindful of individual differences such as behavioral differences, personal faith, as well as cultural and ethnic diversity.

Knowing the worth of an individual is to bear a conviction in their capability of doing well for themselves and bringing about positive change in the world. Social workers help their clients in building this capacity by encouraging self-determination and self-reliance and allowing them to cater to their needs. Social workers are aware of their responsibility in the mutual goods problem. In the mutual goods problem, social workers work to strike a balance between the needs of the client and the community at large. The concept of egalitarianism helps them realize this responsibility and solve the problem.

## Egalitarianism

Social justice is a cardinal principle of social work that is reinforced by egalitarianism, which is the belief of equality for all members of the community.

As egalitarians, social workers can resolve conflicts of interest between clients and the broader society. They work towards equality by generating opportunities for the disenfranchised, marginalized, and underprivileged.

They take social and political actions that ensure guaranteed access for the vulnerable factions of society to necessary facilities like education, healthcare, and employment. For instance, they could help in opening up a job market by retraining programs and setting up advocacy networks against discrimination at the workplace.

Once indoctrinated with the value of egalitarianism, other professional values and principles such as competence, social justice, and integrity (discussed in later chapters) follow suit.

### Professional Objectivity

Objectivity is a broad concept. Some describe it as a belief in an objective world, independent of human experience. It is often associated with traits such as impartiality, detachment, and submission to evidence. Professional objectivity is the practice of this concept in social work.

The 1980s saw mainstream society adopting postmodernism; a Western philosophical movement that engendered notions of relativism, subjectivity, and fostered mass-skepticism. While some academics have associated postmodernism's "person-in-environment" concept as in-line with social work, its effects are hotly contested.

Detractors of postmodernism attribute it with a gaping trust deficit within people, particularly between the masses and social workers. Since the 1980s, skepticism has grown as people began viewing social work as a "subjective effort" for a "subjective cause," leading to a decline in the quality of social work globally.

Therefore, social workers must understand and practice professional objectivity, making it essential to understand two critical psychological concepts: transference and countertransference.

**Transference and Countertransference in Supervisory Relationships**

Social workers are engaged in supervisory relationships with clients and the community, empowering empower and guiding them in making decisions for their well-being. To understand transference and countertransference, think of the word transfer, which means the shifting of something from one place to another.

These concepts help social workers understand the unconscious nature of interactions, particularly with clients who come from severely regressed and violent backgrounds. For instance, social workers with cases involving children being exposed to the risk of non-accidental injury or abuse will inevitably be disturbed as the clients will transfer their emotions onto them.

Similarly, in the field of Psychology, transference is when a client redirects or projects their feelings from an important person in their life (a significant other or a close friend) to the clinician. It is a useful concept to project into social work as well.

Social workers must realize that individuals, families (at micro-level), small groups, institutions (at mezzo-level), and the community (at macro-level) may project their feelings onto them. It is a very natural product of the emotional aspect of suffering.

Countertransference is a natural reaction to transference. It reminds social workers that they are human beings and that transference will inevitably stir their feelings. Social workers can proceed with their work through their emotions by merely acknowledging this.

# Inclusivity

The values of egalitarianism and professional objectivity go hand in hand. Their understanding helps social workers to improve at their job and enables them to be more inclusive.

Modern human society, despite many entrepreneurs challenging and changing social norms, still has deeply embedded traces of discrimination, both blatant and subtle, based on features like race, ethnicity, gender, and sexual orientation.

Therefore, social workers must engage in respectful but constructive dialogue, appreciating and welcoming diversity – making sure their compassion reaches everybody to help build a safe and positive work environment.

Inclusivity can be difficult due to social workers hailing from different socio-economic and socio-cultural backgrounds, requiring an institutional and personal effort to develop and sustain.

## Professional Development Activities

Professional development activities organized at the institutional level not only help in developing essential values like inclusivity, but they also improve and maintain professional knowledge.

Social work is a dynamic and continuously evolving discipline. Different times have different requirements; therefore, workers require constant in-service training to grow with the discipline. Furthermore, licensing requirements must be adaptive enough to match the pace of this growth.

Social workers can enroll themselves for university courses and attend seminars and workshops, with the internet allowing access to online courses, journals, and webinars. There are conferences to which social workers should be encouraged to participate and present their works on such platforms.

Professional development does not just have to be a formal process. Social workers can take the initiative by reading books and other literature to stay updated, as well as listening to podcasts and participating in informal discussion groups. They can carry out networking activities and develop advocacy networks. Also, they can pick up IT skills such as video editing and SEO optimization, to promote their work.

**Client-to-Client System Competence and Self-Determination**

Dealing with client-client and client-society system competence is another critical aspect of inclusivity. Social workers need to indoctrinate their clients with a responsible agency (self-determination) for proper success.

For example, permanency planning is the process of assessing and preparing children living in out-of-home placements such as foster care – it fosters healthy social connections and helps the children into adulthood. But social workers also need to be cognizant of the child's individuality in the process to strike a balance between attributes that are good for the community and ones that are good for the child's self.

Similarly, clients need to make critical financial decisions on their own. Therefore, social workers strive for the financial literacy of their clients as it reduces their dependence on social work intervention.

## The Role of the Self

Social workers must appreciate the importance of the role played by the self in social work. It demands that they utilize their knowledge-base, skillset, and values in social interventions. Quite often, they overlook the importance of individual roles and lose themselves to institutional agendas and visions.

Self-awareness is essential to discharge the role of the self. Psychological studies suggest that many individuals detach themselves from their true selves and attribute their individuality to their false selves. The true self means to be authentic, driven, and spontaneous.

The false self is believed to be a defensive façade that leaves its holders feeling dispassionate and uncompassionate.

By tapping into their true selves, social workers can develop healthy aims and objectives that are true to their identities. Not only does this impart them with much-needed lucidity in their missions and objectives but also a drive. After social workers get to know themselves better, they are in a better position to ameliorate the sufferings of others.

Social workers usually work in environments where they are required to be particularly observant of the subtle gestures, expressions, and behavioral aspects of their clients to diagnose their problem areas and suggest solutions. Looking for these details requires emotional astuteness and intelligence, which a social worker can only acquire once they are aware of the subtleties of their own emotions.

# Social Work; Self-care Principles and Techniques

A natural outcome of heightened self-awareness and lucidity is the realization of the importance of looking after one's s mind and body. The physical and mental well-being of workers is an essential prerequisite for efficient social work.

Social workers cannot be expected to provide compassionate care and guidance to society without first being compassionate to themselves. Therefore, social workers need to understand basic self-care principles and techniques to allow them to look after themselves (and society) in a better way.

## Burnout

Healthcare experts define social work burnout, a natural outcome, as a condition of inactivity. This work is not only labor and resource-intensive, but it is also physically and emotionally enervating. Many practitioners globally leave their practice due to this burnout.

Owing to the uncertain and tolling nature of this practice, social workers inevitably suffer from sleep-disturbance and insomnia – these are dangerous symptoms of burnout and could potentially affect their overall performance and lead to irritability.

Burnouts can also lead to depression, which can cause a lack of enthusiasm towards activities they may have once enjoyed, displaying a lack of patience with their clients, or be continuously distracted by intrusive thoughts.

They can manifest themselves as estrangement from others, which is the last thing a compassionate social worker would want. There can be fear and anxiety along with a pervasive sense of hopelessness – this can lead to the social worker wanting to abandon their cause.

Burnouts can also affect the functionality of social workers by making it difficult for them to separate work and personal time. They fail to make time for leisure and themselves, causing a further downward spiral of their mental well-being.

As for coping mechanisms for all the conditions mentioned above, social workers may end up resenting their cause. They can resort to unhealthy coping mechanisms such as drug and alcohol dependency,  especially possible as an effect of transference and secondary trauma (discussed shortly below).

## Secondary Trauma

Social work involves combatting social injustice, oppression, and violence, and they often encounter victims of first-hand violence who exposed them to their stories.

Psychologically, this indirect exposure to trauma through a narrative or an account can lead to secondary trauma for the social worker.

Professionals debate secondary trauma as being a reaction instead of an actual disorder, despite affecting millions of social workers all over the world. They should be aware of its symptoms and effects and adopt a  healthy practice to stay in touch with their feelings and be vocal about them.

## Self-Care: An Essential Social Worker Survival Skill

Self-care refers to activities and practices which social workers can engage in to look after themselves. It is essential for effectiveness in social work and helps them honor their professional and personal commitments.

Practicing self-care enables social workers to identify potential challenges and manage them healthily. It also allows them to be exposed to their vulnerabilities, such as tendencies for compassion fatigue, secondary trauma, or burnout. Most importantly, self-care teaches social workers balance. It sets limits to the amount of work they do daily or weekly.

Leading a life of equilibrium is essential for the workers to carry out their work with responsibility, dedication, and compassion.

# Chapter 5: Importance of Relationships

Relationships flourish when you invest time and energy in nurturing them. They require commitment, excellent communication, and empathy. Healthy relationships comprise mutually respected boundaries, open communication, trust, and support.

You feel safe while sharing your thoughts and feelings with the other person, without being ridiculed or mocked. You do not feel like you are competing with your friend or partner. These relationships allow you to be your authentic self and to enjoy each other's company. Healthy relationships foster growth and connection in profound ways.

## Strengthening Relationships

Every relationship requires an effort to strengthen the bond and to maintain a healthy connection. Here are some ways you can improve your relationships with friends, family, or romantic partners:

### Open Communication

Having excellent communication is fundamental to strengthening relationships. Being open and honest in your interaction with the other person makes you feel safe and allows the other person to relate with you and build their trust. People feel disconnected from friends or romantic partners when they stop sharing, especially in times of stress.

Sharing your problems and being vulnerable around each other helps in building trust and brings you closer to others. It is especially important to communicate openly and share your feelings when another's actions hurt you, helping you work through your problems with them while maintaining a healthy relationship.

Excellent communication also involves good listening skills. When someone is sharing their thoughts and feelings with you, you must listen to them attentively, without jumping in to give them your advice. Healthy relationships require you to listen to the other person, so they are willing to share and open up more. The key is to be truly present when you are listening and validating their feelings, making them feel they are indeed being heard and understood, without being judged.

Being a good listener also means being fully present and not assuming you know what the person is about to say. You want to make the other person feel you are genuinely trying to understand how they feel and not assuming anything or passing judgment.

In case of conflict, instead of jumping to blame one another, it is crucial to communicate feelings and concerns without being defensive. Communication and listening are an integral part of dealing with conflicts, as blaming creates resentment. Allow each other space to communicate openly and address each other's concerns constructively.

## Mutual respect

The words you use have the power to hurt others tremendously. It is important to respect and treat each other with kindness, compassion, and love. Ridiculing, belittling, making derogatory remarks, and insulting others will weaken your relationship and should be avoided. Respecting each other is an integral part of every relationship.

## Dealing with disappointments

We often set unrealistic expectations for other people that may lead to disappointment. Therefore it is essential to communicate your expectations. Unhealthy expectations include expecting your partner to always cater to your emotional needs, expecting them never to feel insecure, jealous, or fearful, or never triggering you to have conflicts. These expectations not being met make us feel angry, disappointed, and hurt. It is essential to understand that your partner/ friend is not perfect, to give them space to process their feelings, and not to rely on them for your emotional needs.

Your feelings of disappointment are valid, but it is crucial to focus on your partner or friend's positive attributes and the expectations they have fulfilled, helping you overcome negative feelings by focusing on the positive aspects of your relationship.

## Forgiveness

If your friend or partner has hurt you, and they are trying to improve and work on their mistakes, communicate with them. Forgiveness does not imply that you forget what somebody did and stop feeling hurt. It is simply allowing yourself to process your feelings and to give the other person a chance to communicate and explain their doings.

Forgiveness does not mean you will allow the person to hurt or mistreat you again. However, it will enable you to process your hurt and call for new possibilities in the future.

## Honesty and Trust

It is important to trust one another to form a healthy relationship.

Being open about each other's feelings and sharing your thoughts build trust. Being honest and sincere are essential factors for developing one's trust too.

Being honest also means setting boundaries and having mutual respect within a relationship. Openly communicating with your parents is an integral part of a healthy relationship. Being honest about your limitations with your partner or friends can also prevent feelings of resentment or frustration later.

## Support

Mutual support is an integral part of any relationship. Everyone wants friends/partners to support them when they are feeling vulnerable or stuck in a problematic situation as emotional support strengthens relationships.

We can support each other by validating our feelings, being a good listener, not taking people for granted, expressing gratitude, and showing love and compassion.

## Avoid Trying to Fix or Change Others

We often tend to change or fix other people and pinpoint what we perceive as their weaknesses. It is vital to accept another person fully and not force them to change themselves. Instead, we can focus on how to improve and deal with our limitations. People want to be loved and accepted for who they are. Therefore, you must remain supportive and appreciative of their strengths rather than trying to change or fix them.

# Promoting New Connections

Promoting new connections can be challenging if you are not social. Firstly, it is important to focus on others and not yourself as an essential part of making connections is asking other people questions about themselves to get to know them better. You also have to be a good listener and show interest in what they have to say for them to like you. You can share information about yourself, but sharing too much personal information can deter possible connections.

You must be fully present when someone is talking to you, avoiding cellphones and other distractions, asking questions regarding what they tell you to show interest, and trying to mention their stories later to show you remember.

Mentioned below are some questions you can ask yourself when making new connections:

- Do I feel a genuine connection with the person?
- Do I feel good after spending time with them?
- Am I able to be my authentic self around them?
- Is the person supportive and respectful toward me?
- Is the person trustworthy?

You can promote meaningful new connections with people you can trust and with whom you have a deep level of understanding. Good friends accept your authentic self, make you feel comfortable, and respect and trust you. They show genuine interest in your life, your thoughts and feelings, and listen without judgment. We make friends based on shared interests, hobbies, or preferences. You can explore a friend's interests through participating in different activities that help you to know them better. You can make new connections by doing any of the following.

- Join a club of your interest, which can allow you to meet people with similar interests.
- Attend events like art gallery openings, workshops, lectures, concerts, where you can make new connections.

Once you have met people, you should give your connections time to strengthen. Get to know your friends more and be respectful and kind towards them. Being a good listener helps build trust and opening up emotionally. Offer them support just as you would like them to listen and support you.

Treat your friends the way you would want to be treated. Allow your connections to evolve organically by giving them time and not setting too many expectations. It is essential to give space as it takes time to develop secure relationships.

Every relationship goes through difficulties, and people will make mistakes. Having a forgiving attitude allows your friends to make amends and strengthen the relationship.

## Maintaining Existent Connections

You must take time for your existing connections to maintain healthy relationships; small gestures can remind your friend/ partner that you care for and think of them. Little things like sending a card, a note, or dropping off their favorite foods are simple acts that can cheer them up. Calling to check up on your friends/partner every once in a while, can help in maintaining your relationship and making them feel loved.

Planning activities once a while with your friends/family/partners can be a great way of maintaining connections. You can take a break from your busy schedule for meaningful experiences with your friends, family, or partners, such as road trips. It might distract you from day-to-day stressors of your life and allow you to relax with the people you love.

You can share goals with your friends, such as going to the gym and getting healthier together, allowing you to build your relationship and improve your physical and mental well-being.

It is essential to have honest and open communication with your friends. Ask them about the things on which they feel you need to improve that could help in strengthening your relationship with them. Encourage them to share their thoughts and concerns with you, helping you grow and strengthen your relationship.

You can share thoughts and feelings that make you vulnerable, as that builds trust and promotes a strong bond. You can discuss your fears, insecurities, and weaknesses, which make you vulnerable. These acts will encourage others to share and build a strong connection with you, letting them get to know you better will strengthen the relationship.

Checking in with your friends or partner is a way to maintain your connection, asking them follow-up questions allows them to share more of their thoughts and helps in building trust. If you have out of touch for any reason, ask them what has been going on in their life, as this encourages meaningful conversation.

Be present for important events in your friend's or partner's life, especially if they are going through a difficult time, be there to support them in any way you can. Friends need to be present at milestone-events like promotions, birthdays, or anniversaries for support.

With busy schedules and tough routines, it is not easy to keep in touch. However, it is significant to acknowledge the efforts you or your friend makes in reaching out. Appreciate your friends and express your love and gratitude often, as these are crucial factors in flourishing relationships.

Healthy relationships are crucial for your mental well-being. Respecting each other's boundaries allows others to be their authentic selves. By not setting unrealistic expectations, they enable your growth and provide unconditional love and support.

Supportive relationships promote honesty and allow space to express genuine concerns without judgment. Supportive people enable others to share complicated feelings without dismissing them, and they consistently check up on you. These people are trustworthy, honest, and respect your boundaries.

Healthy relationships can contribute to your growth and improve emotional well-being. Therefore, it is important to form meaningful connections and make efforts to maintain these relationships.

# Chapter 6: Integrity and Ethical Principles

Social workers are required to maintain integrity in their profession. The importance of integrity is enormous because it helps individuals be true to their values and beliefs. It allows them to set limits and can help them identify which type of employment settings and clients they are comfortable with, and what specialization they should choose within the field of social work. It allows them to focus their energies and utilize their talents in opportunities that they are more capable of handling successfully, and meeting the needs of their clients without any negative consequences.

When a person possesses integrity, he or she remains true to their beliefs, focusing their work on making positive changes. On the contrary, if social workers do not have integrity, their actions and intentions might not be in line with their beliefs, and they might not be able to engage in their obligations towards their clients fully. Thus, being honest with your values and sticking to what is morally right is an essential requirement of the field.

Social workers have to confront the ethical dimensions of human conduct every day while considering how their decisions are right and wrong because their choices affect other people. They have to determine what responsibilities and obligations they have to fulfill and what kind of individuals they are aspiring to become, or helping others to become. The role of social workers is not just providing standardized services; it involves counseling over different problems and modeling different ways of life. They cannot be neutral in contemporary social issues and make effective decisions regarding them. Social workers must demonstrate a virtuous character, both professionally and personally. Their integrity and morality represent the ethical code that guides their choices and behaviors in the field.

## Morality

Morals are the accepted standards of behavior that help people live in society collectively. It refers to what prevailing societies sanction as right and wrong. Most people have a set moral code that they follow throughout their lifetimes. They can attribute this code to the community they live in and its guidelines. However, morality requires people to prioritize the benefit of the society over their interests.

Traditionally, people or institutions that are indifferent to right and wrong behavior are considered amoral. Morals may vary amongst people of different cultures or religions, but most are universally accepted. These morals have evolved and become the principles that guide the conduct of individuals within a society. They are also used to judge between acceptable and unacceptable behaviors.

Morality is a fundamental concept in social work. Incorporating this into all the services provided by the field, they are supposed to have a clear distinction between right and wrong, with their work and service in line with society's perception of moral and immoral behavior.

## Professional Values and Principles

Principles are a set of beliefs and standards that provide guidance. The field of social work has set values and principles to which all social workers must adhere. Discussed below are some of the most common professional values and principles of social work:

### Acceptance

The principle of acceptance is that all individuals must be accepted regardless of any limitations they might have, as the social worker believes that the crux of all services is to accept the needs of others. Thus, social workers must not condemn or be hostile towards a client because of behavior or circumstances, but rather acknowledge them and establish a professional relationship by accepting them as they are and not how they would prefer them to be.

### Confidentiality

The principle of confidentiality is an essential aspect of social work. Any professional help or relationship between the social worker and the client must be within the boundaries of confidentiality. Clients have the right to privacy regarding their personal information, and any agencies or individuals who are working professionally with clients must adhere firmly to this principle.

### Self -Determination

This principle emphasizes the client's right to self-determination. It states that every client has the right to choose the appropriate course of action for themselves without social workers forcing any decisions on them. Instead, they are required to support the client's choice and help them develop insight regarding the best solution for their social situation. Social workers should involve a client's requirements while recommending solutions to them.

### Non-Judgmental Attitude

This principle requires that social workers begin their professional relationships with clients without any bias or prejudice. They should not form a personal opinion about the client and decide their worthiness as they should be impartial and provide their services to any client that may approach them without being influenced by the judgments or opinions of others.

## Communication

The principle of communication states that social workers should have enough skills to comprehend the client's needs and requirements. Any misunderstanding between the two can lead to negative consequences, which must be avoided. It is, therefore, essential to sympathize with the client and understand their situation fully before finding the appropriate course of action. Social workers are required to find an effective way to communicate with their clients openly, making them comfortable so that they feel at ease and can express their needs without any hesitation, leading to a better and more comforting solution for the client.

# Dual Relationships and Related Ethical Issues

Ethical issues are common in any professional field, and social work is no exception. Understanding these issues from different perspectives can be multifaceted with the ongoing debate of the concept of dual relationships in the professional field of social work. Professional boundaries, if not appropriately defined, can have serious repercussions, especially concerning dual relationships as they not only hurt the clients but can also the social workers and the profession itself.

There have been a growing number of lawsuits filed against social workers due to misconduct and exploitation.

The Code of Ethics of Social Work has stipulated that if dual relationships become exploitative, they should be discarded. Exploitation is very easy in this line of work as social workers hold a more powerful position than their clients.

Dual relationships can take different forms and be open to interpretation. It not only consists of sexual relationships between social workers and their clients but can have more subtle factors such as developing a friendship, participating in social activities together, belonging to the same advocacy group, or accepting goods as repayment instead of money.

Practices such as engaging and forming personal relationships with clients can create serious dual relationship problems. Clients might feel powerless in front of their caretakers and give in to their demands out of fear,  or feel pressurized into an activity in which they are not comfortable, or forced to pay the social worker illegally. Social workers must adhere to their values and avoid such dual relationships as their purpose is to help their clients and not gain advantages from them. Social workers can prevent all such ethical issues by following the Code of Ethics and pledging to work towards the welfare of society rather than catering to their self-interests.

## Method Generation for Evaluation

Social workers are accountable to their clients, programs, funders, policymakers, and the profession itself to ensure that they deliver the best services according to their capacity. Thus, there is an expectation that they evaluate different policies, programs, practice interventions, and research activities to ensure that they are contributing to the real purpose of serving people.

There are many methods to evaluate the effectiveness of social work, which can be conducted at micro, mezzo, and macro levels of the field. The four most common methods of evaluation of social programs are the following:

### Scientific experimental model

These models emphasize objectivity, accuracy, data reliability, and targets objectivity. It uses scientific methods to evaluate social programs, which are usually experimental and quasi-experimental in design and focused on a particular goal having an underlying theory that guides it.

### Management-oriented model

Management-oriented models are developed for specific evaluation needs. Their primary emphasis is on the comprehensiveness of the evaluation, which includes assessing the broader context of organizational performance. Such models are more often used to evaluate social work agencies and institutions.

### Qualitative Anthropological Model

This evaluation strategy is more focused on the importance of observation and places particular emphasis on the value of human subjective interpretations in the evaluation process.

### Client-oriented model

This assessment strategy places the clients at the center of the investigation as it evaluates their satisfaction with the service or program. The evaluation of social work activities most commonly use this method.

# Chapter 7: Competence

## Defining Competence

Competence is defined as the capacity of a person to understand a situation and his knowledge, experience, and skills to act reasonably. Being a competent social worker is one of the core values of the profession. Competence allows social workers to acquire knowledge, apply theoretical concepts, assess situations, and act with accuracy. A social worker plays many roles as the profession demands they go beyond merely meeting the minimum criteria and continue to strive towards professional and personal excellence. The challenge for social workers is to try to be better than the previous day while working to promote the values, rights, and dignity of the people they serve.

Since social workers serve the most vulnerable citizens, their clients have unique interests, skills, and composition. Thus, social workers must be competent enough to confront the changing requirements of their clientele and enhance their abilities through research, reading, and other formal educational opportunities. Such activities help increase awareness and offer a fresh perspective for delivering services and resources to clients in need.

Competent social workers employ a collaborative approach by engaging with professionals in other fields as well as clients from different walks of life. This approach helps them develop more interest in engaging individuals, groups, families, and entire communities who are the victims of social injustices—making oneself more competent increases the value of a professional social worker immensely.

Competence includes any skill, knowledge, or behavior that results in the empowerment of others. Social workers need to engage in a continuous process of learning and self-improvement with activities that would help build personal and professional skills include mentorship programs, spiritual practices, and self-help education.

It is essential to understand that society is continually changing, and social issues have never been more diverse than they are now. Expanding competence to encompass these various dynamics, developing a vast knowledge and expertise related to the world is critical to serve others.

## Education and Training for Social Work

Being a professional social worker requires formal education and training to become competent, with the minimum qualification being an undergraduate degree in social sciences or any related field. They are required to sit a licensure exam depending on which state they want to practice their profession, while some states, within the US, issue entry-level licenses to individuals who have earned a bachelor's degree in social work.

Social workers who aspire to advance in the field and provide clinical services require a postgraduate degree in social work or any relevant doctoral degree. They are also required to pass their state's social work licensure exam to begin professionally. Other related fields include sociology, psychology, and development studies.

There is an added requirement of field experience that has substantial weightage in graduate degrees as it is an essential aspect within the field of social work. Social workers require hands-on experience and training to become acquainted with the everyday aspects of working in the professional field. Fieldwork can be done under the supervision of the university while getting your degree.

Social work aspirants will have to pass standardized examinations that are administered by the Association of Social Work Boards to meet the states' licensure requirements. They are also required to have direct service hours supervised by a licensed social worker, to meet the license's requirements.

After the approval of the license, social workers can begin their job search and start working. Standard employment settings for social workers include local agencies, nonprofit organizations, private practices, religious establishments, and community advocacy groups. Social workers must remain updated with the best practices in the field through continuous efforts towards learning. They can enroll in different courses online or join workshops to enhance their skill base and knowledge, allowing them to find better jobs.

## Utility and Development of Professional Skills

Social workers need to develop a professional identity. Defining this professional identity can be as the internalization of skills, knowledge, professional values, norms, behaviors, and the goal of social work to perform at micro, mezzo, and macro-levels of the profession and focus on social justice.

The process of developing a professional identity in social work starts with acquiring adequate knowledge and skills. It then leads to one's understanding of the profession and the values and beliefs associated with it. Finally, you incorporate all these steps with personal values and create a unique identity for yourself within the profession.

Developing professional skills is not limited to education or fieldwork but a combination of the two and is a never-ending process. Field education helps the development of stronger professional identities for social work through experiences challenging students perception of social work practices, and this allows them the opportunity to address any challenge with their perceptions and knowledge.

For students to successfully develop professional skills through their education, they must be given the opportunity of self-assessment, reflective supervision, and favorable relationships between instructors and students, thereby allowing the experience to be more meaningful. These students can be better professionals playing different roles in the social work field ranging from generalists to serving society at multiple levels.

## Utility and Development of Personal Skills

The profession of social work requires a diverse range of emotional, professional, and cognitive skills. Many have a natural aptitude for these demanding skills; however, it is significant to enhance them throughout your career, and social workers must pledge to become life-long learners, which is one of the ethical requirements for professional social workers. But while professional skills are fundamental, the profession requires some personal skills too, which makes workers better and more competent in their field.

One of these personal skills is the ability to listen as most of the social workers' role consists of listening to their clients effectively. They have to reflect on what their clients need from them and have engaging conversations with them to ensure that their problem is understood. Being a good listener builds up a trusting relationship with the client and makes them feel comfortable while building up a therapeutic alliance with them. The client feels seen and heard and can place their trust in the social worker's abilities to help them solve their problems.

Having high emotional intelligence is a personal skill that is very useful to a social worker; this includes having a high level of self-awareness, compassion, empathy, and sensitivity toward others. It enables social workers to perform their duties well by relating to and caring about their clients' problems. Emotional intelligence is a necessity for a competent social worker.

Social workers are not only engaged in helping clients directly, but also have management and administrative duties. To perform such functions, they must have excellent time-management skills to ensure that they fulfill all their responsibilities. Organizational skills are crucial in delivering services like clinical case management or psychosocial support. Moreover, the ability to think creatively is vital to come up with new and innovative solutions for social problems. It allows social workers to help their clients in a variety of situations and issues that they may be facing.

Another significant personal skill is being culturally responsive. Social workers engage with a great diversity of clients, thus needing to be open towards different cultures, religions, and traditions and be respectful towards the people of all beliefs. Openness is a personal skill that may separate an excellent social worker from an average one.

Social workers might often feel they have not done enough and that their work is never complete, which can cause emotional and mental stress in their personal lives. It is essential to have the ability to deal with such stress and pressures; otherwise, it may have a negative impact on their personal lives. Setting appropriate boundaries can help to avoid such situations. Engaging in self-care activities while creating a healthy work-life balance can help social workers lead happier and more content lives, which will improve your professional life.

Being hardworking and dedicated are also requirements for this profession. You can face the inevitable setbacks and obstacles, but having the courage not to give up and continue to strive for the benefit of others is what makes the personalities of social workers so unique. Developing these personal skills is thus essential for being a competent and professional social worker.

# Chapter 8: Social Justice

## Defining Justice from a Social Perspective

The simplest definition of justice is fairness. Social justice is fairness or equity that manifests itself in society. Implying fairness in education, healthcare, employment, housing, and all fundamental human rights as any sort of discrimination is not compatible with the concept of social justice. This idea is widely used today, but its emergence can be dated back to the 1780s, and the term has been commonly associated with economics since the Industrial Revolution. However, the modern definition of social justice is not limited to any one facet as it includes all aspects of society and is closely related to human rights.

Social justice is dependent upon four essential principles, which include human rights, access, participation, and equity.

### Human Rights

There exists a strong association between social justice and human rights. Social justice can only be achieved if all members of society can get their rights, as a fair society respects and protects the rights of all individuals. They cannot be considered just if any members are deprived of their rights.

### Access

Access to necessities of life such as food, shelter, and education is central to a fair society. Restricting this access due to factors like race, gender, or class, causes severe discrimination and suffering for some individuals or segments of society. A socially just society provides nondiscriminatory, equal access to every member.

### Participation

Another principle of social justice is to allow participation from every individual in the society. The voices of the vulnerable and marginalized segments of the community are often neglected, not being permitted to voice their opinions or participate in any decision-making due to a lack of power. It further creates inequality and obstacles; therefore, participation from all members must be encouraged and rewarded to obtain social justice.

### Equity

Equity has significant importance in the concept of social equality. Equity means all effects of discrimination are taken into consideration to aim for an equal outcome,  by giving the most vulnerable segment of society more resources so that it can be similar to all other segments to maintain equality in society.

Social justice is not confined to choices regarding the distribution of resources, but it considers how societal institutions are structured to guarantee equal rights for all. It aims to ensure opportunities and meaningful social participation for every individual.

In the context of social work, social justice has different philosophical approaches, namely: utilitarian, libertarian, and egalitarian. These approaches offer a different perspective used to make informed decisions regarding the society or the allocation of resources.

The utilitarian theory emphasizes actions that bring the most significant benefits and the least harm for the majority of the people. Here the rights of individuals can be ignored if they meet the interests and needs of the overall society.

The libertarian theory states that individuals are legally entitled to any or all resources that they have acquired themselves. It rejects the notion of equitable distribution of resources and stresses on individual autonomy. This approach focuses on protecting personal freedom and propagates minimal support from the government or state.

The egalitarian theory states that all members of society be treated equally. Providing all members with equal rights, opportunities, and access to resources, which should be redistributed within the society to uplift the most vulnerable members.

## Identifying Social Injustice

Social justice seems like it would be a straightforward concept to implement. However, in today's society, the situation is quite the opposite. Numerous social justice issues are prevalent in countries around the world. The utopian ideas of social justice are far from reality. Social injustices occur at every scale and in many forms, whether it is the discrimination against an entire culture or teenage bullying in the school hallways.

The key to identifying such injustices is to investigate how people are suffering around the world, which opportunities they are being denied, and why some people are so disconnected. Let us look at some examples of how and where social injustices occur today.

### Discrimination

Many people around the world are discriminated against based on their race, creed, religion, language, culture, or identity. Examples of racial discrimination are present in history and today. For example, slavery was a significant form of racial discrimination, which existed in the 1800s, forcing African Americans and other people of color into servitude. Today, about 40 million people remain trapped in some sort of slavery or forced labor, which deprives them of a better way of life.

Another type of discrimination that exists is ageism. Older people are denied the right to employment and other benefits because of their age, seeing them as a burden to society and forcing them to retire or replacing them with younger individuals in many employment settings.

**Wage Gaps**

There is a noticeable difference between the wages earned by men and women, with women being paid less than men for the same work. We can break this wage gap further for minority men and women who are paid less due to their ethnicity or sexual orientation. The fact that some are paid less because of their gender is an injustice.

**Lack of Opportunities**

Our world has not been able to provide equal opportunities for every individual. Many children in developing countries do not have access to quality education. In many countries, boys are preferred over girls due to social norms and miss out on getting educated and building a career. Healthcare systems around the world are vastly different, and not every sick person can get access to quality healthcare facilities, as the rich are favored while the poor are left to suffer. Employment opportunities are also minimal, forcing many children to work in factories or sweatshops for minimum wage.

Such injustices plague the world today, and many suffer at the hands of the society in which they were raised.

## Effective Methods to Achieve and Maintain Social Justice

Keeping in mind the various issues that exist in society today, there is a great need for people to strive towards social justice. The role of social workers comes to the forefront in addressing these social injustices as they have the tools that are required to understand the power dynamics that hold the world. They have to be aware of how to advocate for justice using different programs and policies by engaging the stakeholders. The role of a social worker is to fight against injustices by involving themselves in counseling agencies, public education systems, community organizations, nonprofits, and government institutions.

Social work schools prepare social workers to strive for justice through policy practice and advocacy, empowering their clients to advocate for social change on behalf of communities or vulnerable groups. The most common approach is the unified model of policy practice. In this approach, social workers ask their clients to become agents of social change to try to advocate for change and address different societal issues. They are then encouraged to make broader changes that impact entire communities. This approach believes in empowering individuals to help address clinical issues with generalist practices, creating positive changes in the client's own lives as well as the lives around them.

Another approach for social workers to maintain social justice is through policy advocacy, involving working on behalf of vulnerable groups to advocate for policy changes. This approach entails advocacy work by lobbying elected officials, building coalitions to address specific social issues, or by working with agencies to inspire change. A variety of activities such as meetings, public gatherings, news agencies, petitioning, and engaging stakeholders can be used by social workers to push for change.

Creating an equitable and socially just society is a very long process requiring constant efforts, not only by social workers, but by governments and the general population. Fighting for social justice does not only involve the economy but includes grassroots issues such as low wages, discriminatory practices, and lack of opportunities in different sectors of the economy. Social workers need to engage themselves at all levels to address these deep-rooted problems. The general population needs to become more aware of their rights, voice their opinions, and take collective action against the institutions that are threatening the sanctity of human rights around the world.

# Chapter 9: Micro-Level Social Work

## Defining the Micro-Level

As previously discussed, social work is a broad discipline, and the field is divided into three main categories, namely the micro, mezzo, and macro levels. While mezzo and macro social work involve activities at a higher level, micro-social work pertains to one-on-one counseling services for people in need. It is the most common type of social work and has a longstanding history in the professional field. To define micro social work is working with individuals, families, or small groups to provide support and services to those clients who face challenges and injustices in the social system. Clinical social work is also included in this category because it deals with clients in a therapeutic capacity. Included are other non-clinical services like providing access to resources

Social workers who work on a micro-level deal with the most vulnerable individuals in society, including children, young adults, disabled people, victims of domestic violence, older people, and students. They provide support services such as housing, mental health services, therapy, or healthcare. These social workers perform their services at the grass-root level to pull individuals out of their suffering and enable them to be productive members who contribute to society. Micro-level social workers directly interact with their clients. Thus, the field of social work starts at the very bottom level and broadens to include larger groups and communities until an entire society is affected by its practices.

Individuals working at this level of social work are rewarded for applying the broader social work theories on a personal level to make a significant difference in the lives of their clients. This profession is usually much more rewarding compared to other professions, as they can directly observe their results. Hence, people who have excellent interpersonal skills and a passion for improving the welfare of others are more suited to work at the micro-level of social work.

Micro social work can take different forms depending on the underlying philosophy and perspective of the social worker. Some may prefer to help resolve personal problems, others may place their focus on the social relations that are causing the problem, and some may choose both of these approaches simultaneously. Micro-level interventions are directed towards creating change in interpersonal relationships amongst individuals, families, or smaller groups. However, it is essential to note that not all micro social workers focus their efforts on changing individuals only. They may target other systems like changes in the physical or social environment, which would, in turn, may facilitate the enhancement of the individual or family in question.

Social workers who want to work at the micro-level are required to be knowledgeable about interpersonal, group, and family dynamics. They must know about human development, the psychology of human beings, and how environmental factors influence the decision making of people. They require specific clinical skills such as questioning, active listening, counseling, crisis intervention, empathy, and mindfulness.

**Examples of Micro-Level Social Work**

The following examples are provided to gain a better understanding of social work at the micro-level. A clinical social worker supports clients through therapeutic activities in a mental health clinic and engages with individuals or small groups in therapy sessions.

A military social worker supports soldiers and war veterans to cope with post-traumatic stress disorder. These social workers engage in activities such as counseling and providing support to veterans and their families. They also help their clients gain access to exclusive benefits such as state-funded education or health facilities.

A medical social worker is employed at a hospital or healthcare facility working with sick patients to provide them access to health insurance and other benefits. They may also offer counseling services to critically ill or patients with acute diseases, helping them cope with depression and survive through difficult times.

A school social worker provides counseling services to students who are victims of mental health problems such as depression and anxiety. They may also help resolve conflicts in the school regarding bullying or harassment. They are often engaged with students and their families to help them solve their issues.

# Norm Entrepreneurs and the Power of Individual Change

Cass Sunstein coined the concept of norm entrepreneurs in 1996. He defined a norm entrepreneur as someone interested in changing the social norms in a society. He stated that the social conditions existing today are fragile as they are dependent on a set of social norms to which many people in the society might not agree.

However, there is a segment of the population that is interested in changing the underlying social system and make efforts towards shifting the societal norms that define them.

Norm entrepreneurs can be individuals, governments, or any societal actors, dedicated to uprooting the existing laws and values that govern society. These norms result in various forms of social injustice that the population must face. They try to take it upon themselves to break the traditional values and instill new norms that are better suited to the needs of all individuals in society. Norm entrepreneurs are only successful when the majority of people are inclined towards making efforts to change the existing system and incorporating new norms that promote social justice in their everyday lives.

Understanding that a society consists of many different actors, and each actor plays a role in the system. Reforming societies has to include efforts from every actor in the system.

While it is true that society and its institutions can transform individuals, individuals can also bring about changes in society and evolve their institutions. As this interaction between individuals and society takes place throughout different generations, individuals and cultures are mutually shaped by each other. Developing an altruistic society is necessary to evaluate how individuals in their capacity can contribute to this process of development.

Social change starts with personal transformation. It leads to commitment and motivation that is required for absorbing this change into people's lives and the community. For example, children who grow up in societies where charitable values and cooperation are encouraged, are more likely to incorporate these values into their lives and behaviors. This change will not be momentary as it will reform how the child conducts himself when he grows up and throughout his life, thereby transmitting these values to his children, and so on. Their brains and genes will evolve to create intrinsically, altruistic beings in the future. This dynamic process of influence and change will continue throughout generations that follow.

The behavior of an individual might not affect the society directly. However, certain habits and values instilled in individuals may have a positive or negative impact on the overall society. When individuals try to modify or reform society by displaying positive habits and behaviors, they create a social impact.

Change begins with how individuals conduct themselves and interact with other members of society. The first step to lead such a change is to open yourself to differing opinions and voices of those around you. Listening respectfully to people's ideas and problems can create awareness regarding our society. Accepting the differences amongst each other and learning that a myriad of perspectives exists in society is crucial to help resolve social issues.

Participating in real change requires individuals to have difficult conversations that give rise to meaningful solutions. Accepting the injustices of the society and ignoring the vulnerable populations is going to feed the status-quo. Individuals from all walks of life must come together, listen to each other, have conversations, unite on points of agreement and act on those to help create positive change in the social system, which reflects the values and norms of the people.

Over the years, there has been immense progress in the fields of human rights, women's empowerment, justice, democracy, solidarity, eradication of poverty, and discrimination amongst people. However, there is still a lot to be done. These global issues may seem like only people in positions of power can only resolve them. However, never underestimate the power of an individual.

Personal transformation plays a massive role in facilitating more significant changes. Change always begins at the micro level until they mature into encompassing the global level. Micro-level social workers recognize this fact and dedicate themselves to transforming society, one step at a time.

# Chapter 10: Mezzo-Level Social Work

## Defining the Mezzo-Level of Social Work

Conducting social work at the mezzo level is on an intermediate scale. This level falls between the micro and macro levels. That means that it involves advocating for and serving neighborhoods, institutions, or other small groups of the population. Social workers at the mezzo level help out different communities to resolve their issues and improve the welfare of society as a whole. They are involved in other micro or macro social work activities that help solve the problems of individual clients in tandem with larger social groups.

Mezzo social work consists of working with groups of people. These groups can be small and intimate such as employees of a company that requires conflict mediation and resolution services, or they could be larger groups with people in a support group or drug abuse recovery patients. The role of a social worker working at the mezzo level varies in different employment settings. For example, social workers who serve in schools, hospitals, community centers, or prisons are involved in mezzo social work. Other examples include group therapists, community service managers, business social workers, and clinical social workers.

Social workers who serve at the mezzo level of the field are focused on changing groups or organizations and resolving issues at the institutional level rather than at an individual level. They can play different roles to achieve this goal. Social workers can act as facilitators for groups or institutions to function correctly, which may involve strengthening relationships amongst the members and enabling group decision-making processes. Many social workers who work at the mezzo level have experience with micro or macro-level work, which involves a more direct approach towards individuals or interventions at a larger scale.

For example, a therapist might be directly interacting with a child in school and may find that his problems are due to his family background. They would be inclined to get involved with the family and start working to develop their bonds. The therapist is performing at both the micro and mezzo levels simultaneously.

### Importance of Mezzo Social Work

While the fundamental aspects of social work at all levels are the same, mezzo level social work may require some different services from social workers due to its differing nature. The responsibilities and roles of the social worker at various levels are somewhat different. The main focus of social workers who work on the mezzo level provide their services to a variety of clients such as small or medium-sized businesses, local organizations, schools, communities, and other small groups. Instead of focusing their efforts towards individual change, these social workers direct their efforts towards promoting cultural or institutional changes, requiring substantial experience with interpersonal relationships as well as community engagement.

Specific mezzo level organizations also exist. An example is the Family Equality Council, which was created for making policies that help families be respected and given equal opportunities to succeed in society, targeting minority group families who may face discrimination. Organizations that work for social issues such as foster care, adoption, employment, housing, healthcare, and education exist. Some are focused on inclusive education for all children and achieving work equity for their parents. They also advocate for legal equality to encourage supportive communities.

## Examples of Mezzo-level Social Work

Generally, mezzo level social workers are engaged in social work interventions with formal groups or whole organizations. Some examples of formal groups or such organizations are listed below:

- Team groups
- Interdisciplinary task forces
- Community service clubs
- Self-help groups
- Task-oriented groups
- Social service agencies
- Educational systems
- Correctional facilities
- Healthcare organizations
- Nonprofits

Social workers at this level are focused on midlevel intervention. The process of change at the mezzo level takes into account the functions, roles, structures, decision-making patterns, and interaction styles amongst the group members. The group or organizations needs are met by drawing resources from individual members and the wider society.

Social workers who work at the mezzo level of social work must understand the dynamics of these formal groups and be able to facilitate change amongst them as it is critical for the development of quality services and social programs. They require skills such as decision-making, organizational planning, and conflict resolution. Social workers must understand the group they are working with to come up with better solutions for their problems. The three most common groups that mezzo social workers engage with are:

## 1. Families or Household Groups

This group consists of members living in the same household that might include children and older people. These groups are most effective when the interaction between families is a pivotal component to resolve the underlying issue. Social workers may work with multiple families at once to create a larger group where each family is considered to be an individual entity.

## 2. Therapy groups

These are groups of individuals not from the same family or who have had any relationship beforehand, only knowing each other through the group setting. All members are part of the group to seek individual assistance, and any interaction amongst them is for therapy purposes. There is no objective of the group apart from receiving therapy—for example, an anonymous group of people who are trying to recover from substance abuse or alcoholics.

## 3. Peer or Self-help groups

These groups consist of individuals who have common problems or interests. Such groups are formed with the belief that interacting and working with each other will open up more opportunities for all the members and help in instilling change. For example, a group of students and other young people start working together to help the elderly with groceries.

Mezzo social work is critical in handling matters using group or teamwork. Problems like addiction, loss or bereavement, unemployment, chronic illness patients, marginalized discrimination, can be solved more effectively if a more significant number of people are involved. These problems cannot be solved by interacting with few individuals since they affect many people. It is foolish to assume such issues can be resolved on a one-on-one basis. Thus, mezzo social work brings people with similar problems together to share experiences and ideas that can help solve them.

## The Family Unit: A Building Block of Society

Families can be considered the building blocks of society as they create well-integrated members and instill societal values and norms into them. It not only gives individuals status in the community they live in, but it also offers material and emotional security to its members. Thus, families are essential in determining the role of an individual in the overall society. It helps members build different skills and acquire knowledge regarding how the world works. They also provide support and care for more vulnerable individuals.

The role that families as units can play in the development of a society is crucial as it can result in positive or negative consequences. Sometimes families accept the status quo and work towards maintaining it, contributing towards the continuance of social injustices within society. Factors like inheritance, social capital, and education are crucial in determining the place of an individual in society. Hence, wealthy families are more privileged and immune to social inequalities than families with minimal resources, who are usually left to face the injustices of the world.

The community benefits when families are healthy as healthy families produce productive members who contribute to the welfare of the community. Family values motivate people to work towards improving the lives of those around them. They are more compassionate and take responsibility for others. For example, parents are more likely to get involved in community projects than people who live alone. They set an example for their children to get involved and take action to resolve societal problems.

The role of parents is especially important because they care for the future generation that is going to impact the existing social system. Parents make strong efforts to provide the best education and care for their children, grooming them to be better citizens.

Another aspect of families contributing to society is to help meet the basic needs of individuals who cannot meet their needs themselves. They do not discriminate against minors, the elderly, the disabled, or any vulnerable individual.

Families are the fullest reflection of the strengths and weaknesses of the society they live in at the very grassroots level. They are important agents of development and change that have a substantial impact on the overall social system. They not only contribute towards the continuance of the society through procreation, but they also ensure that society keeps functioning through socialization. Therefore, concentrating efforts to improve the welfare of families in society is an essential goal in the field of social work.

# Chapter 11: Macro-Level Social Work

## Defining the Macro-Level

Macro-level social work involves the broader community and system-level functions. Social workers who work at the macro-level are engaged with large groups of people, entire communities, cities, or major institutions. These social workers are usually not involved in one-on-one interactions with clients, such as a patient-social worker relationship. However, many social workers at the macro-level have previous experience with micro-level work, as it is the root to identify interventions and solutions for more significant societal issues that are faced at the community level.

The macro-level of social work involves professionally guided interventions and practices that are specifically designed to instigate change in the community, organizational, or policy arenas. Macro practices are far-reaching beyond individual responses and are dependent upon the needs, issues, and concerns faced by the overall society at large. It is addressing community problems and requirements within a broader context, which affects the issue, the population, and the society or organization. Dealing with such issues also requires sufficient awareness regarding the political context of the problem and its potential consequences.

The objective of macro-level social work is to cater to the needs of whole communities, which can be determined by geographic locations like cities, towns, neighborhoods. These communities are large groups such as religious communities, political groups, cause-driven groups, or international organizations. Macro social workers play a variety of roles to help such groups overcome certain obstacles and work towards the provision of resources and practical solutions. They may take on various roles within the field, such as policy advocates, community organizers, lobbyists, professors, program developers, or research analysts.

The field of macro social work encompasses several activities, which includes social work research, organizational development, community educational initiatives, program development and evaluation, advocacy, policy analysis, or nonprofit administration and management. These activities are also essential to achieve the goal of social justice. Due to the focus on macro-level policy changes and fighting against unjust government policies, the field of macro social work helps build healthier communities and provides an improved standard of living amongst the people in general.

Macro social workers may be involved in activities like organizing community efforts, leading development initiatives, working with government institutions to address national issues, designing interventions for poverty reduction amongst many others. They may also work for solving other social issues, such as human trafficking, that are faced on the global level. Macro social workers are also often involved in policy work from the grassroots level, all the way to large-scale lobbying activities at the top. Macro-level social workers are more often involved in the following activities:

**Investigating social issues**

Social workers are involved in research and community outreach programs to identify the various social issues that are affecting the community.

**Developing programs for marginalized groups**

Social workers develop and manage different initiatives to assist the most vulnerable communities and groups. These programs could target any specific issue like the provision of adequate healthcare or creating support programs for veterans.

**Advocating on behalf of the underprivileged**

Social workers work on behalf of the disadvantaged populations in society. They help in the provision of necessities to these groups by lobbying for changes in the legislation or engaging with government officials to resolve systematic issues in society.

**Educating people**

One of the tools for social advocacy is to educate people and create awareness regarding existing social problems. Social workers are involved in many educational initiatives to teach the population about their fundamental rights and the societal injustices that are prevalent. They also use educational materials for the distribution of information to the broader community.

**Examples of Macro-level Social Work**

Social work at the macro level is essential in the mission of the field to improve the welfare of all people in the society with particular attention to the problems and needs of the vulnerable and poor populations. The impact of activities like social work research, community education, program development, and political advocacy have far-reaching consequences. Thus, macro-level social work is central to the direct practice of the social work field.

The conceptualization of macro-level practices in the field of social work has evolved over the years. Since the origination of the field, social workers have shown flexibility and innovation in creating the roles and responsibilities concerning the demands and needs of the changing society.

The most common example of social work at the macro level is that of policy analysts and advocates. Social workers who are playing these roles are involved in raising awareness of the systematic problems that, in turn, are negatively affecting individuals. They are also working towards the development of macro-level strategies that address these social issues on a large-scale. For example, a forensic social worker performs many duties such as collaborating with other social workers, paralegals, and attorneys to give expertise in the development of initiatives to help children and young adults in judicial or welfare systems.

They can also be working as policy analysts at nonprofit organizations and other human rights groups, policy think tanks and law firms. These social workers are usually part of interdisciplinary teams that work with human service organizations to instigate legislative and social changes to raise the welfare of the people.

## Coordinating with Agencies and Organizations

The concept of service that is central to the field of social work transcends all borders and limitations. Social workers on the macro-level may be required to work with international organizations that involve traveling to far off locations. The need for social workers arises when conventional support structures like governments fail to address the problems of the people. Social workers step in to not only help people with the provision of their basic needs but also to design and formulate such systems dedicated to serving the needs of the people that will endure the test of time.

Social agencies and human service organizations usually employ social workers to help meet their goals, as they are always engaged in some capacity with such organizations in their professional lives. Coordination with such community organizations is essential in the macro practice as these organizations have the resources and capabilities to enhance the lives of larger groups of people.

There are different types of community organizations with which social workers engage, such as voluntary organizations, informal groups, or professional service agencies. Such entities include schools, churches, healthcare units, social service groups, fraternities, and other clubs. Most are nonprofit and frequently advocacy-oriented, allowing social workers to collaborate to help in the application of community-organizing strategies to accomplish their mission.

Some organizations are service-oriented and usually have a more extensive resource base than volunteer organizations. Social workers coordinate with such institutions to make use of the ample resources and direct them towards the most beneficial activities for the society.

Social work is commonly practiced within a particular organization, the duties and roles being dependent on the nature of the organization and those with which they are collaborating. For example, social workers who are engaged in family-oriented volunteer organizations may be involved in counseling work.

Social workers have unique skills to offer to such human service organizations. The accumulated body of knowledge regarding social issues enables them to understand the problems of individuals and communities within their political and social contexts. They are also able to promote the values and principles of the field of social work and take political stances on behalf of vulnerable populations. Social workers collaborate with such organizations by taking part in a wide range of activities such as counseling, networking, developing policies, research, and critical thinking. These unique skills raise the abilities of social service organizations, and can play a role in societal welfare,

The role of social workers in these organizations is not limited to the macro-level but also involves micro and mezzo level practices. In terms of macro practices within the organization, social workers are commonly involved in setting organizational goals and policies, developing social policy and legislation, raising funds for the organization, and designing the ethical frameworks in which the organization is to operate. Thus, the collaboration between community organizations and social workers proves to be very fruitful.

The importance of such organizations in social work is immense, as without them fulfilling the objectives of providing social welfare would not be possible. Since there are different issues that the society currently suffers, various organizations have emerged around the world that are targeting these dynamic issues. The collaboration between social workers and community organizations is significantly contributing to the development of sustainable communities across the globe. They are working hand in hand to ensure a better and more stable future.

# Chapter 12: The Interconnectedness of the Micro, Mezzo, and Macro

If you want to help others and bring about a positive difference in a person's life, social work is the right path for you. Social workers play a crucial role in helping families, communities, and individuals. However, the advantages of social work cover a broad scope under three levels: Micro, Mezzo, and Macro.

## Consolidating the Three Levels of Analysis

By investing sufficient time and adequate resources, social workers can consolidate the three levels to create a more significant impact. You can move your way between the micro, mezzo, and macro levels or work with them simultaneously by combining two or more levels.

Let us discuss this through an example. As a social worker, you help those who are suffering from mental illness or psychological issues and interact with them one-to-one. This type of help is referred to as a micro-level of social work as you are providing individual assistance.

Your client is dealing with anxiety or depression and find that the family could be having a hard time dealing with the situation as well. You broaden the scope of the social work you do and extend your services and assist the family by helping them adjust and get through this challenging time. You provide useful tips or information that will benefit the family overall by advising them on how to cope with stress. Hence, by going out of your way and extending your services to the entire family, you will enter the mezzo-level of social work.

By using the same example, you can also move to the macro level on the scale by reaching out to the community or elsewhere and talk about the importance of the effects of mental health and how many people overlook it.

The above scenario describes the three levels of social work and how you can move from one level to another. However, the scope of macro social work extends to a much wider circle than illustrated here.

## Interdisciplinary Nature of Social Work

The interdisciplinary nature of social work involves combining the knowledge and skills of different areas, collaborating with various professions, and working closely to enhance skills and gain a broader perspective.

The knowledge of social work is influenced by other disciplines such as psychology, child studies, and human behavior. Interdisciplinary relationships are essential to excel in this profession and for the service to be effective. Individuals from various professions come together and work in the same environment to form relationships and exchange information. For example, a group of people with completely different professional backgrounds may meet regularly to discuss the complexities of specific incidents or cases.

Exchanging of ideas will benefit disciplines of entirely different backgrounds, and is a good step towards the professional development of social workers. Social workers dominate the structure of social services and are more suited towards collaborating with the underprivileged or the disadvantaged in society. A social worker is required to practice their knowledge as long as it is relevant to the field, and exchanging this knowledge is part of a social worker's identity.

## Methods of Networking

Social work gives you a sense of accomplishment because you help people in need, inspiring others to do well and work together for the betterment of everyone. By advocating and forming bonds with different groups of people such as clients, families, communities, and even other professionals, social workers also get a chance to improve themselves and learn new things daily. There are different groups that social workers can connect with:

- Individuals and families
- Small communities or groups
- Other professionals
- Society at large

Here are some ways in which social workers can reach out and build their network:

### The Elevator Pitch

The elevator pitch is a 30 to 90-second speech in which you describe yourself and talk about what you do and how you can benefit the other person. The elevator speech should have a natural flow to catch the attention and interest of the other person. You can talk about your goals and what you wish to accomplish in life to leave a positive impression. It is an excellent tool for networking and a unique way to connect with different people. You can also ask other people about themselves and what they do to engage them in a conversation.

## Meeting Up for a Cup of Coffee

Social workers can meet for a cup of coffee or lunch to bond with people, as an informal meeting and usually makes the other person feel more comfortable while talking. At a micro-level, this works exceptionally well as it makes the client feel like they can connect better. It will help you determine the nature of the problem and provide the best solution for addressing it.

## Social Networking Sites

Social media is a great way to connect with various people globally. LinkedIn is the most popular professional social network where individuals from different professional backgrounds form connections with one another. There are other great networking sites, such as Facebook. Facebook gives you the option to create groups or pages where you can add people and interact with them. You can have multiple groups suited to the different types of people to whom you can offer your services.

## Volunteering

Nothing shows how committed you are to the wellbeing of others more than engaging in volunteer activities. Various organizations offer membership and to volunteer readily, allowing you the opportunity to connect with different people, including other social workers, as well as the people who may need your help.

## Social Networking Events

There are various seminars and webinars social workers can attend where they meet new people and exchange ideas. Seminars and speaker sessions offer public participation, where people get to know each other and share their thoughts and ideologies.

Attending a conference or an alumni event is a great way of networking. You will be able to enhance your skills, and others will have a chance to get to know you better.

## Useful Tips for Networking in Social Work

Social networking is enjoyable, as well as rewarding. Although you cannot become an expert in just one day, time and patience allow you to improve at work.

## Stay Focused

One of the essential traits of a good social worker is their listening skills. Staying focused and attentive is a sign of excellent listening skills. Over the years, the people you speak to may not be able to recall where you met, but they will remember how intently you listened to what they had to say.

**Don't Shy Away from Helping**

Let people see how much you want to help them by letting them know you are there for them and allowing them to express themselves to you. Social work is all about helping each other, and a great way to do that is by letting people know that you can.

**Share Information**

Networking is about exchanging knowledge and sharing ideas. Talk to different people and express yourself by telling them about your interests and vice versa. Sharing information will help you learn new things.

## Methods of Record Keeping

The Social Work Dictionary (2014) defines recording as, "the process of putting in writing and keeping on file relevant information about the client; the problem; the prognosis; the intervention plan; the progress of treatment; the social, economic, and health factors that contribute to the situation; and the procedures for termination or referral." The recording is an integral part of social work practice for various reasons:

1   It helps in your learning and development as you can reflect upon your previous work and correct any mistakes in the future, or you can find new solutions or methods while dealing with situations.

2   The method of record-keeping helps in effective communication among social workers. Most social workers have to work in shifts and keeping a record of their work for the next social worker to update them regarding the events of the day.

3   Record keeping is a part of the Code of Ethics and values associated with the profession.

4   Social workers are required to maintain transparency with their clients and are professionally accountable to the organization to which they are associated.

5   Relevant information is stored and kept safe to facilitate in improving the quality of service.

6   In later years the recorded information may be used for research or teaching purposes.

## Important Guidelines for Record Keeping

### Code of Ethics

A social worker must ensure that ethical values are not overlooked or violated in any way while maintaining a record. Some ethical values include an honest service to humanity, integrity to your profession, social equality, confidentiality, and client confidence.

### Social Work Interventions

Social workers can maintain intervention records in a file, by electronic means, or both. The recordings must not include irrelevant data that does not meet the needs of the clients or add any value to the service.

### Client Disclosure

A social worker has the responsibility of informing the client about what is being recorded, how the recording will be used, and who will have access to the information. It is necessary to have the client's consent before commencing any form of relationship.

### Complete Information

The recording should contain complete information relevant to the case, such as the client's contact details, consent, progress, any new problems arising during the relationship, and commencement date.

### Ensure Confidentiality

The social workers are responsible for ensuring that the recordings are kept in a secure location and inaccessible by any unauthorized individual. All parties involved must be informed about their rights, and agree on the confidentiality clause before the commencement of services.

### Clarity of Context

If you are maintaining a record of your writings, it is crucial to ensure that the written content is explicit and easy to understand. Avoid using jargon and complicated words that some may not be able to comprehend.

### Facts and Opinions

As a social worker, you must ensure that you do not mix facts with opinions. It is against the code of conduct if you form a judgment based on someone else's opinion. For example, people have different views on various subject matters, such as whether a person suffering from mental health problems should be allowed to be alone or not.

### Types of Recordings

### Narrative Recording

Narrative recordings describe real-time or ongoing events. They represent a scenario according to the way we speak, as if in the form of storytelling.

### Verbatim Recording

This record-keeping method provides the exact description of the interview. It is an account of everything that each party involved had spoken during the session without any changes or fabrications.

### Process Recording

Process recording contains details of the session but with paraphrasing. This type of record only keeps the relevant information. It preserves information according to the sequence in which the series of events or sessions took place.

### Summary Recording

This type of recording is useful for distinguishing important facts from the entire session. It is a carefully drafted summary of the narrative as a whole. The advantage of summary recording is that it reduces excess data and irrelevant information by filtering out the facts.

## Consultation Approaches

Consulting is a process in which social workers seek advice and expert opinions from fellow social workers or consultants who are specialized in the field and have more experience. The consultant often engages social workers to help them identify and correct any mistakes in their practice.

They may help them look at a problem differently and find better solutions. Consultants also impart knowledge to polish the skills of new social workers.

The social worker and consultant agree on a mutual basis about the duration of consultation, the mode, and the functional area that needs to be the primary domain of discussion. Social workers should seek clinical consultation from a member practicing the same profession. However, they may also request a consultation from other professionals with a different set of expertise.

What level of qualification is required to become a consultant?

- Specialized training in the field
- Substantial clinical experience
- Additional training or mentorship

## Consultation Procedure

Professional development through consultation is usually conducted on a one-to-one basis, in groups, or with people from similar backgrounds and social circles.

Individual sessions can meet specific target driven learning outcomes and usually last for about an hour, but this may be subject to change as per the agreement.

Group sessions focus on a particular group to address the training needs of the social workers. Social workers then have the advantage of learning from one another's experiences and the consultant's skills and practices. It helps reduce the level of stress and isolation as you get to share stories about how you overcame particular challenges and are dealing with different situations at work. Group sessions save time and are cost-effective.

A consultation session with people from the same professional background who share a similar level of proficiency and knowledge is much better suited to supporting and encouraging one another.

## Supervision in Social Work

According to NASW, "Supervision is the relationship between the supervisor and supervisee that promotes the development of responsibility, skill, knowledge, attitudes, and ethical standards in the practice of clinical social work. The priority of the supervision process is accountability for client care within the parameters and ethical standards of the social work profession."

## Types of Supervision

Supervision is considered a mandatory activity for the professional development of social workers. The following functions or types of supervision that can be used individually or combined to be more productive.

## Administrative Supervision

Administrative Supervision is required to meet the requirements of the organization, and optimum work performed.

### Educational or Clinical Supervision

Clinical Supervision develops the expertise and abilities required for sound judgment, proper clinical knowledge, and skills, including self-reflection, and attitudes essential for performing clinical tasks such as psychotherapy. Clinical Supervision helps social workers understand the code of ethics and values, and it also hones the learning capacity of an individual.

### Supportive Supervision

It is using supportive supervision that improves the morale of social workers by providing encouragement and support. It is not much different from administrative or clinical supervision, but it has the added function of increasing job satisfaction and reducing work-related stress.

## Methods to Inform and Influence Organizations

Social workers possess the skills to advocate their knowledge effectively and positively influence organizations. For example, a clinical social worker has command of the subject and will easily be able to preach to organizations about the importance of self-reflection or self-awareness.

How a social worker informs or influences an organization is different for each individual as everyone has a different capacity for learning. For instance, you need to have a firm grasp on the teachings of clinical social work supported by an ample amount of training or mentorship to back your case. Organizations will not engage social workers who are not proficient or capable of doing what they set out to achieve.

The members eligible to join the organization may include students, practicing professionals, and experienced clinical social workers. How you can connect with organizations is by visiting their website and leaving a message, via email, or phone. It all starts with small steps, and you gradually work your way to the top.

## Potential licensing and Accreditation Options

A licensed clinical social worker is a trained and qualified psychotherapist who assists individuals in coping with the challenges of mental health and everyday life problems. Their overall function is to improve the quality of life and help people find their way out of social and psychological issues. A social worker should have a Master's Degree in Social Work and studied subjects such as sociology, individual psychology, mental health theory and practice, and human behavior.

As a professional social worker, you can choose one of the following programs:

**Bachelor's Degree in Social Work:** it is the minimum requirement to qualify for a job as a social worker. It includes majors in psychology or sociology, and an individual with this degree will be eligible for an entry-level position.

**Master's Degree in Social Work- MSW:** This is a requirement for clinical social work as well as other health settings. Most jobs in public and private sectors, such as a training position, demand a higher level of degree.

A Master's Degree qualifies the social worker to advance in the respective field and enhances the skills to perform clinical examinations and psychoanalysis. Thus, potentially being able to take on a supervisory role and explore new horizons of social services to assist your clients. A Master's Program is generally about two years, inclusive of field experience or internship.

**Doctorate in Social Work- DSW or Ph.D.:** A profession of college or university teaching usually requires a doctorate. It needs intensive research work and extensive social work experience to be successful.

### Licensed Clinical Social Worker- LCSW

An LCSW must have an MSW, DSW, or Ph.D. Social workers must have command over mental health treatment by observation, account, evaluation, interpretation, intervention, and treatment. It allows them to modify behavior through social work guidance and methods and processes to treat emotional and mental health. The process of becoming a licensed clinical social worker comprises the following. Please note that the process may vary for different states:

### 1. Register as an Associate Clinical Social Worker (ASW)

To become an ASW, applicants must obtain a Master's Degree in Social Work for credibility in a program. Once the applicant has received an MSW, they may proceed to complete the ASW application.

### 2. Sufficient Work Experience

The candidate must have at least 3,200 hours of supervised social work experience throughout a specified period, dedicating at least 2,000 to areas such as psychological treatment and diagnosis as well as counseling services.

### 3. Required Course Work

The applicants must have completed a few extra courses as needed to qualify for being a Licensed Clinical Social Worker (LCSW). Some of these areas of study include child abuse, domestic violence, and professional ethical conduct.

## 4. Applying for LCSW Licensure and ASWB examination

The mandatory requirements for the application form, fee submission, and examination clearance must be fulfilled as specified. You will be eligible to apply for an initial license upon clearing the exam and meeting all the requirements.

# Chapter 13: Theories in Social Work

Many theories guide social work practices. These theories provide general explanations that are backed by evidence and data obtained through scientific methods. Theories provide an explanation regarding human behavior and the interactions amongst them.

Since the basic unit of social work are the people, social workers must understand how these people behave and what external factors influence them. Thus, social work theories help in understanding the clients and their needs more profoundly and equip social workers with insight that is necessary to provide adequate services. These theories are derived from extensive research and practical evaluation. The social work profession draws upon these theories of human behavior, development, and the social system to investigate complex situations and facilitate individual, organizational and social changes.

This chapter takes a look at some of the most common theories applied in social work practices and their backgrounds.

## Conflict Theory

Conflict Theory is a significant paradigm in the field of sociology. It also supplies some of the critical components of the social work profession. This theory provides a detailed explanation of how differences in power amongst members of the society can influence the lives of individuals and entire communities. This theory explains how power structure and disparity can give rise to several social problems.

The division of power in society is unequal. Certain groups or individuals emerge dominant over others and try to assume control over the social order through manipulation and authority, advancing their interests at the expense of society's, perpetuating different forms of injustice and oppression amongst vulnerable populations not provided the same influence. For example, this power differential can lead to income inequality or racial discrimination.

The Conflict Theory views society as a place of deep-rooted inequality that creates constant conflict between classes resulting in social change. The fundamental concept of the theory is that the structure of the society benefits a few groups at the expense of others. Moreover, factors like gender, race, class, and age contribute to social inequality. Conflicts arise between the minority and dominant groups, and these conflicts are vital in achieving social change by addressing the differences in power relations.

### Association with Karl Marx

Conflict Theory was constructed by Karl Marx, who is considered the father of social conflict theory. Marx envisioned that the conflicts within society would become the primary source of change as they emerged consistently throughout history in times of revolution. The source of these revolutions resulted from the domination of one class over the other. He named these classes the bourgeoisie, who were the powerful owners of resources, and the proletariat, who were the oppressed working class. He stated that these classes were directly facing each other to create two hostile camps, causing interruptions in periods of stability, which would eventually lead to social change. According to Marx's theory, conflict instead of consensus amongst the members of society leads to social change.

### Application to Social Work

Conflict Theory helps inform social work interventions of who is disadvantaged and who benefits from the existing social arrangements. It helps identify the sources of societal issues like oppression, marginalization, discrimination, and inequality in wealth. Thus, allowing social workers, in their client assessment and intervention strategy at the macro, mezzo, and micro levels, to address the difference in power dynamics in society and confront the sources of the underlying conflicts.

For example, if applying Conflict Theory to the micro-level of social work, social workers would work towards creating an acceptable level of co-existence between peaceful society members and gangs. Similarly, at the macro level, social workers use the Conflict Theory to understand the battle between the society and the LGBT community. They would then work to assist the LGBT community in obtaining their fundamental rights and protection. Thus, conflict theory can be utilized by social workers in various scenarios to help oppressed groups battle with dominant ones. The goal of social workers is to overcome conflicts between the two groups and create a balance of power amongst them for the welfare of the overall society.

## Development Theory

Development Theory refers to the collection of ideas regarding how societies can move towards positive change and is incorporated in the field of social work. It includes concepts like modernization, which is the idea that economic development can lead to improved equality and more job opportunities for people.

Social development is central to this theory. Focusing on the eradication of poverty in society involves a macro policy perspective. The theory provides the context in which the process of development takes place, promoting a joint approach in which all sectors of society work cooperatively to achieve social welfare and improve the standard of living. All sectors of the economy should interact and work together to achieve the best results for society as a whole. Social workers are deeply involved in this role as they engage with healthcare workers, agriculturalists, engineers, and program developers. The concept of community development emphasizes the participation of local people in providing different services. It is an approach that places focus on the empowerment of the community through education and awareness, capacity building, and community organization. The method is a bottom-up strategy that eventually impacts the entire society.

## Erik Erikson's Eight Stages of Development

Erik Erikson was a German psychoanalyst and the creator of the psychosocial theory of development. This theory is central to social work practice as it considers the effect of family, society, and other external factors on the personality of individuals during their lifespan. Erikson's theory states that individuals have to go through eight interrelated stages of development. The theory further explores multiple aspects of identity, including the ego identity, personal identity, and social identity. The eight stages are defined as:

## 1. Infancy

In the first 18 months of your life, you are defined by the nurturing ability of your mother and father, taking the form of visual contact and touch. In this stage, the child develops many qualities like confidence, optimism, and security if he or she is provided with an adequate environment, without this, he or she might develop other conditions like insecurity, mistrust, and worthlessness.

## 2. Early Childhood Years

During the second stage, which starts after 18 months until the age of three, the child builds characteristics like self-esteem and autonomy. They also learn other skills and how to differentiate between right and wrong. Well cared for children more confident and carry themselves with pride, while other children might show defiance, stubbornness, and temper tantrums. It is a vulnerable age for them, and they might sometimes feel inadequate or shameful at the inability to learn new skills.

## 3. Preschool Age

In this stage, children have the desire to copy the adults around them. They become more imaginative and create certain situations in their head, inspired by real-life occurrences. Preschoolers are generally more experimental and become more aware of our relationships with other people, especially our families.

## 4. School Attending Age

From the ages of 6 to 12 years, the latency period starts. In this is the stage children are actively learning new skills and knowledge, and developing a sense regarding the various industries. This stage can also be considered as a very social stage of development and can result in unresolved feelings and severe self-esteem issues due to negative experiences. As children start interacting with other children in school, they find new people from which to draw their knowledge, and parents no longer remain the only authority over them.

## 5. Adolescence

In the stage from ages 12 to 18, is where the situation starts to change. Development no longer depends on what happens to the individual but instead on what the individual does himself. Adolescents start struggling to find their own unique identities in the world and have to face many struggles and negotiations. They are exposed to a variety of social interactions and develop their sense of morality. They become more affiliated with their ideals, causes, and friends.

## 6. Young Adults

At this stage, individuals start looking for companionship and love. Young adults start settling down to start families. They seek intimate and satisfying relationships, and if unsuccessful, they might feel loneliness and isolation.

## 7. Middle-aged Adults

In this stage, people become more focused on their careers and their families. They are faced with a bundle of responsibilities, and they may even attempt to take on more significant roles in society to improve welfare. People at this age are fearful of being inactive and not doing something meaningful, which can result in significant shifts in their lives.

## 8. Late Adults

Adults over the age of 65 till death are mostly involved in reflection. Some adults look back with pride and integrity and knowing that they have led meaningful lives and positively contributed to society. While others may have a sense of despair due to the failures, they may have encountered.

# Racialization Theory

The concept of racialization describes the processes through which racial identities are produced. It emphasizes on the dehumanizing and racial meanings related to a specific group, social practice, or unclassified relationship. The racialization theory explains how some groups are categorized into races, which previously were not considered as a specific race.

## Distinguishing between race and ethnicity

The concept of "race" refers to the physical differences amongst different groups and cultures, which are considered significant in society. They are distinct groups of people within the human species. Racial characteristics are usually physical such as the color of your skin, eyes, hair, or your facial structure. All human beings belong to the Homo sapiens species; however, genetic variations have occurred over time, which has triggered different physical appearances in the species. However, some scientists are of the view that all human beings belong to a single race, namely, the human race.

On the other hand, "ethnicity" refers to shared cultures such as ancestry, practices, language, and beliefs. It often depends on the geographic region of people. Members belonging to the same ethnic group usually identify with each other based on some common traits. Some examples of ethnicities are Irish, Jewish, or Cambodian. It is solely based on the behaviors of people rather than their physical appearances. People can belong to mixed ethnicities.

Most researchers share the belief that the concepts of race and ethnicity are socially constructed as their definitions are continually changing over time and are merely dependent on public opinion. More importantly, the idea of different races due to genetic differences has brought about the concept of racism. Based on race, people begin to divide themselves into being more superior or of an inferior race. However, this is also done based on ethnicity.

## The concept of race and marginalization

Racism is a huge obstacle to the integration and cohesion of the overall community. Discrimination based on race and other racial abuse leads to social marginalization or alienation. The term marginalization refers to socially excluded groups of people and minorities. As a result of this exclusion, individuals and communities that are the victims have to suffer from inaccessibility to various resources and opportunities, and being prevented from participating in the social and political system of society.

In the existing social systems around the world, the term marginalization encompasses a long list of populations and cultures which include the LGBT community, senior citizens, cultural minorities, military veterans, less intelligent individuals, physically disabled people, people with chronic illnesses, poverty-stricken groups, sex offenders, and the homeless. In short, any member of the society who seems to be different in any way may become the subject of marginalization.

Throughout history, race and marginalization have had a strong association. The most significant example of this can be demonstrated from the pre-American Civil War era. At that time, African Americans were marginalized, taken as slaves, and considered to be inferior due to the color of their skin. They were denied opportunities like education, healthcare, and employment while being treated with disregard and disrespect, and hate crimes against the group were prevalent. Once the call for emancipation was taken up, there were various disagreements from those in American society, which led to war. The American Civil War enabled the victimized group to live as integrated and respected members of society. However, certain issues can still be seen today.

It is apparent from the racialization theory that any type of discrimination against populations based on their race or ethnicity will always be a significant obstacle in the development of any society. Preventing a segment of society to participate in the economy can never result in positive consequences. On the contrary, these acts cause oppression, which eventually leads to lobbying, protesting, and resistance to bring about change in the existing system.

Nowadays, there are a large number of outreach programs for social minorities in almost every sector. They range from scholarship opportunities in universities to employment opportunities for cultural minorities. Efforts like this help promote diversity and social cohesion, build acceptance of different races and cultures, and create cooperation amongst people belonging to different regions of the world. These people overcome their differences and work together for the betterment of the overall community.

## Grounded Theory

The Grounded Theory is a systematic method commonly used in social sciences. It involves the construction of theories by a methodical accumulation of data and analysis. One of the fundamental concepts of social research is to investigate human beings and their behaviors, and how factors like knowledge, values, and identities govern these behaviors.

This research approach makes use of inductive reasoning instead of scientific methods. Grounded theories are used in research studies beginning with a question, initiated with the collection of data. Researchers review the collected data, which leads to the formation of repeated ideas or concepts. These repeated concepts are tagged with codes and taken from the data. These codes are then grouped into concepts and then into categories, eventually leading to the basis for a new theory. The Grounded Theory is very different from traditional research methods as it is used to study new concepts related to social development and welfare.

**The Importance of Real-Time Data**

The Grounded Theory approach starts with the collection of real-time data, which is vital in the creation of new concepts. The collection of this data is done through methods like conducting interviews, using open-ended questions, participant observation, focus groups, or by studying artifacts and old written materials. The quality and accuracy of data should be ensured during collection to obtain more reliable results, which cannot be based on the concepts or ideas of the researcher but rather depend on the method of collection and analysis. Hence, all analyses must be done as soon as the data collection process is complete.

After the data collection process, researchers then code the data in a detailed manner called microanalysis. The interviews of the study population are coded to help develop a list of ideas or concepts to study further. They then critically analyze the data to ensure that all the hidden trends and meanings become apparent as this is a qualitative process. The researchers then name the segments of data with different labels to categorize, summarize, and account for each piece of information.

Although Grounded Theory has many different approaches, some aspects are common in all of them. For research to be "grounded," it is crucial to follow these methods:

- Coding – This includes categorization and the labeling of data.
- Discovering social processes or concepts in the collected data.
- Deriving abstract concepts through induction.
- Using theoretical sampling to simplify the categories in the data.
- Bridging the gap between writing and coding with analytical memos.
- Integrating the categories into a theoretical framework.

# Rational Choice Theory

Rational Choice Theory is a framework that models the social and economic behavior of individuals. Renowned sociologist George Homans founded the theory in 1961. The basic concept of the theory is that the aggregate behavior of society is the result of the behaviors of individuals who are making individual decisions. The theory explains what determines these individual choices and then makes assumptions regarding these decisions. It assumes that all individuals have a set of preferences amongst the choices available to them, giving them the ability to pick an option they prefer. Consolidating all individual choices helps explain the behavior of the overall society.

# Understanding Human Behavior and Economic Models

The role of economics in determining human behavior is undeniable as most human behaviors are motivated by money, profit-making, or cost avoidance. People usually calculate the benefits and costs of any decision before they make it. This concept is called rational choice and forms the basis of the rational choice theory.

Numerous economic theories and models try to conceptualize human behavior. They explain how the production, distribution, and consumption of resources is dependent on money. The Rational Choice Theory incorporated the same principles to explain how human interactions occur in society. According to the theory, the motivation for individualistic behavior is derived from personal needs and desires. As they cannot obtain all things, they are required to make choices amongst available options, calculating the outcomes of each course of action and determine which option is the best. Such individual decisions are considered rational decisions, and rational decisions give the highest satisfaction to the individual.

The theory sees that all social actions are rationally motivated, and further assumes that individual actions determine complex social phenomena. This process is known as methodological individualism, and it states that the basic unit of social life is individual action. To understand social change and institutions, we must understand how they arise due to the actions and interactions amongst individuals in that society.

## The concept of predicting choice patterns

At the individual level, the theory specifies that individual agents choose the outcome or action that they prefer the most. In decisions where the choices can be evaluated in terms of its benefits and costs, the agent will choose the outcome, which provides the most significant net benefit to him, i.e., the benefit minus the cost.

This theory can also be applied to general settings and actions which do not have any direct costs or benefits. The Rational Choice Theory consists of choosing the most rational alternative from a set of actions or objects. The main priority of the individual is to determine what the best outcome is for himself.

Two technical assumptions are made about the preferences of individuals:

**Completeness** – This means that if an individual is faced with two options a and b, he will either prefer a to b, b to a or is indifferent amongst the two options. Hence, all pairs of alternatives are comparable to each other in this way.

**Transitivity** – If the individual prefers alternative a to b, and alternative b to c, then he will also prefer alternative a to c.

With both of these assumptions, the rational choice theory can be applied to any set of exhaustive and exclusive actions. Individuals rank the actions in terms of their personal preferences rationally and consistently and then make a rational choice.

Rational Choice Theory is only one of the theories that social workers can apply to understand their client's behaviors and guide them towards choosing the best intervention that would help them. For example, cognitive behavioral therapy is a popular choice of social intervention for clinical social workers in helping their clients realize the importance of rational purpose behind their actions. It also helps them change their behavior to serve a more rational purpose.

## Global Systems Theory

The Systems Theory states that individuals should not be seen as islands but should be viewed as the components of larger groups, societies, organizations, and families. It further explains that individual problems are created and influenced by many factors in the individual's social ecology. Their behavior is affected by numerous factors that all work together as a system, such as parents, friends, school, wealth class, and home environment, which play significant roles in influencing the thoughts and actions of individuals. The theory helps to seek the ineffective parts of the system, which will create a positive impact overall.

Systems theory advocates that social workers must always observe and analyze all systems that may contribute to their client's behavior and wellbeing, targeting their efforts towards strengthening those systems. Providing their clients with therapy or positive role models that lead to the creation of more supportive social systems.

### Human Systems

Systems theories provide social workers with an understanding of social issues that may arise in human systems like families, neighborhoods, and communities. These include family problems, child abuse, low self-esteem, and community dysfunction. An example of how systems theory can be applied to human systems is the family systems theory given by Bowen. Bowen developed eight concepts of family systems that are all interrelated. These are effective in strengthening the functioning of families.

Other models, for example, the life model, are also based on the systems theory. It helps examine how individuals fit in with their environment and how they adapt to limitations and toxicity present in this environment. This model can be applied in the context of organizations or communities, enabling clinicians to investigate the crucial experiences in their client's lives, which impact their development and behavior. These experiences may include major life transitions, stages of increased stress, or changing relationships.

The model also incorporates how historical events and major societal changes determine different generations.

Systems theory also helps to observe multiple social systems and the different levels of social environments, i.e., the micro, mezzo, and macro systems. At the micro-level, family systems and individual relationships are studied. At the mezzo level, organizations and institutions are viewed. While at the macro level, society-wide factors, like laws and cultures, form the basis of human behavior.

## The Concept of Interdependency

The concept of social interdependence is also central to the Systems Theory. It explains how social systems are defined by the type of interdependent relationships amongst its members. The essence of social systems is that this interdependency can lead to the group becoming dynamic, which means that any change in the condition or state of one member impacts the state of all other members.

The members in a system are made interdependent through their common goals. It is contingent upon how each member can influence other members during any interaction between them.

How these common goals are structures also determines how members interact amongst themselves and whether the interaction is positive or negative. Positive interdependence occurs when the goals of individuals are intersecting, meaning that they are only achieved if members work together. On the contrary, negative interdependence occurs when individuals can only obtain their goals if they have to compete with the other members in the system.

The knowledge and application of the Systems Theory in the field of social work is essential as it offers social workers special insight that can help them provide better services to their clients. It can help them break a client's harmful habits and put a stop to behaviors that are an obstacle towards them achieving a better life. Social workers can help clients understand how to better navigate through the social systems in which they live. This theory allows professionals to think about the various dynamics that are faced in society and how they can contribute to positive change.

The social work profession includes taking into account the different facets of human life. Systems Theory provides a unique way of addressing how people behave in terms of the relationships amongst people and their environments. It emphasizes that an effective social system can only be formed if all its members are aware of each other's needs, expectations, and behaviors.

Social work involves taking into account many factors of an individual's life. While there are many theories in social work, systems theory is a unique way of addressing human behavior in terms of these multi-layered relationships and environments. The theory is premised on the idea that an effective system is based on individual needs, rewards, expectations, and attributes of the people living in the system.

## Transpersonal Theories

Transpersonal theories explain the experience in which an individual's sense of identity goes beyond the individual himself to include broader aspects of human life, mind, and spirit. The theory suggests that beyond the ego of individuals, some developmental stages involve experiences of interaction with some external phenomenon. These stages can stimulate the highest qualities in human beings, including creativity, wisdom, and altruism. These theories help understand the full potential of human beings and help to develop it amongst individuals.

### The Spiritual and Transcendent Aspects

Transpersonal theories stem from transpersonal psychology, which is the study of the transcendent or spiritual aspects of human beings. It also helps explain issues like human development, mystical or peak experiences, and the probability of developing beyond the boundaries set by one's ego. It focuses on human experiences, which are transpersonal.

The profession of social work integrates transpersonal theories as it relates to human thought and behavior. The spiritual aspects of these theories should not be confused with religious aspects. They include all sets of practices and beliefs that help individuals develop personal insight, growth, and development in their lives. The spiritual aspects of humanity offer insight and help develop new perspectives for social workers.

Some essential aspects of the Transpersonal Theory are that it emphasizes the spiritual aspects of people regarding the society in which they live. It also recognizes the importance of spiritual and religious support systems for understanding client experiences, which may help them achieve a sense of social and personal fulfillment. These transcendent aspects play a key role in defining the inner strength and personal growth of individuals as it helps people apply values and develop morality in their daily lives. Another important aspect of this theory is that it includes the process through which cultural, societal, and environmental factors contribute towards human suffering.

Some social workers believe that using transpersonal theories is in line with the primary goals of the social work profession. The Transpersonal Theory has direct meaning in the context of family and children centered social work. They focus on the welfare of individuals, as well as the welfare of the overall society. If the transcendent and spiritual aspects of life are neglected, then the goals of the profession would not be achieved. The theory provides a non-sectarian framework for social work that is spiritually sensitive. Recognizing that religious and spiritual diversity is vital as diversity helps practitioners address how human behavior is formed in a better way.

Social workers can make use of transcendent theories to address many practical social issues like adverse childhood experiences, divorce, mental illness, youth development, chronic disease, hospice, social work education, human service organization, or aging. These theories push the boundaries of conventional social work and include all spiritual traditions and practices. It helps to create structural change amongst individuals and communities by making efforts to expand the consciousness of individuals as well as society.

Social workers must incorporate this approach as it may prove to be a fundamental aspect of their client's lives, and may ensure that the services they are providing help their clients become better members of society.

## Socialization Theory

### Defining the Socialization Process

Socialization is the process that explains how humans learn throughout their lives. It is the process of internalizing the values and ideologies of society, including learning and teaching, which ensures the continuity of social and cultural norms. Socialization is a significant influence on the beliefs, actions, and behavior of all people, thus linking the theory to developmental psychology, which states that human beings need social experiences to develop their culture and to survive.

### Understanding Socialization and Societal Issues

Socialization plays a crucial role in acquainting individuals with the standards of a specific social group or society. It teaches people how to function within the group by illustrating the expectations. Teaching children the expected norms of the society they live in, results in the shaping of the kind of individual they will become when they grow up.

Similarly, the process is essential for adults who join new social groups, as socialization helps transfer the norms, beliefs, and values of the new group to them. Socialization can lead to desirable outcomes such as morality in society. Individuals are influenced by society's consensus on what they find acceptable, and this induces socially acceptable behaviors.

The Socialization Theory refers to a general process, but it is important to note that socialization usually occurs in specific contexts. Culturally specific means that people from different cultures get socialized in various ways as their values and behaviors are all shaped differently.

Human beings are naturally social creatures with social interaction being central to their development, and the socialization process facilitates this development. However, if it fails, it might have some negative consequences, such as social deprivation. Social deprivation occurs when people are deprived of the usual engagements with the rest of society. Some groups are more likely to be socially deprived, such as people with mental illness, poverty-stricken groups, less educated people, and people who have a low socio-economic status.

Research has proven a distinct relationship between social deprivation and human development. Humans pass through critical periods in their lives during which they experience certain environmental factors that stimulate their growth. When interaction is deprived, and they are socially deprived, this hinders the process of development for them, and they get left behind.

For example, feral children display the effects of severe social deprivation as they grow up without meaningful social interactions, may have experienced abuse by their families, been kept in isolation, or abandoned at a young age. Hence, these children fail to develop language skills and have minimal knowledge about society causing them to behave differently and become outcasts who cannot be rehabilitated.

**Tragedy of the Commons**

The Tragedy of the Commons is an economic issue in which individuals have an incentive to consume resources at the expense of others. As they have no way to exclude anyone from consuming the resource, overconsumption, underinvestment, and the eventual depletion is the result. Individuals create demand for the resource above its supply, so every person who consumes an additional unit of the resource prevents others from obtaining it. Thus, people neglect the welfare of the overall society in the pursuit of self-interest.

According to this phenomenon, the problem of overpopulation is the same. People are becoming more selfish and demanding more resources and do not care if all members of society can consume those scarce resources. The Tragedy of the Commons can be applied to many situations. A typical example is climate change and pollution. If the environment is seen as a global resource, people are not limiting the amount of pollution they are producing and are consuming this resource at a fast rate. The result is climate change, which affects the global population. Due to the selfishness of a few members, everyone will suffer.

# Psychodynamic Theory

## Psychoanalytic Ideas of Sigmund Freud

The Psychodynamic Theory explains the personality of human beings in terms of consciousness. It includes conscious and unconscious forces like desires and beliefs. Sigmund Freud proposed the theory according to which the personality of individuals consists of the id, the superego, and the ego. The central concept of this theory is that childhood experiences significantly shape the personality of an individual. This theory is commonly linked with psychoanalysis, which is a type of therapy that helps reveal unconscious thoughts and desires of people.

Freud was the founder of the psychoanalysis method to treat mental illnesses and to explain human behaviors. He places particular emphasis on the childhood experiences of individuals as they have a significant influence on personalities. An example to illustrate this phenomenon is that anxiety, which originates from trauma in a person's childhood, remains hidden in their consciousness and can eventually lead to neuroses problems in the latter part of their life.

The theory states that human beings explain their behaviors deceptively with their conscious mental activity, trying to hide their true motivations. It does not mean that they are deliberately lying; instead, that human beings are not able to understand when they are deceiving themselves as well. One of Freud's most impactful ideas was to model the mind and divide it into three layers.

The first layer consists of the conscious mind where an individual's current thoughts, feelings, and focus exist. The second layer is the preconscious or subconscious layer, where memories live. The third layer is the unconscious mind, which is the deepest level of the brain; this includes all primitive and instinctual desires and a repository of all the processes that drive human behavior.

Freud further developed a more structural model of the mind that coexists with the ideas of unconsciousness and consciousness. He divided the mind into three segments:

**Id** – This operates at the unconscious level focusing on the desires and drives of the individual. It includes two key drives. The first is the instinct of survival, which helps individuals engage in activities that sustain life. The second is the death instinct, which drives individuals towards dangerous and violent behaviors.

**Ego** – The ego of an individual acts as a check for the id and works to meet the need of the id in a socially acceptable way. It is linked with reality and developed from childhood.

**Superego** – the superego is the portion of the mind which consists of principles and morality. It encourages individuals to act in morally acceptable ways.

## Psychodynamic Theory and Social Work

Social workers and psychoanalysts have worked together with various groups of patients and have engaged in advocacy practices for them. Some social workers use psychoanalytic practice to help treat patients with mental illnesses. It can be applied in a variety of ailments such as addiction, sexual deviance, and schizophrenia. The method can be adopted for helping out vulnerable children and adolescents who are suffering from various issues.

The theory fully incorporates the values of the social work profession. It focuses on the collaboration between clinician and patients and emphasizes the ability of people to change and grow into better individuals. It helps understand the complexity of interpersonal relationships amongst various members of society.

Various psychoanalytic approaches are used to treat patients in a wide range of situations. For example, they are used in short and long-term therapies, helping to uncover past traumas and experiences of patients to understand their current situation and behaviors better.

# Chapter 14: Major Practice Models of Social Work

Theories, as discussed earlier, provide social work with fundamental references concerning its greater objectives. But theories are too abstract if not molded to work with the pragmatics. Therefore, it makes sense to attempt the translation of social work theories into the more tangible practice models. Theories provide the analytical framework upon which models rest. Models may be considered "representations of structure."

The choice of models in social work is arbitrary – this is because there is no consensus within the discipline about drawing distinctions between the models. A better way to conceptualize these models would be to think of them on a spectrum.

## Therapeutic Relationships

Politicians, lawyers, administrators, social activists, police officers, community organizers, doctors, nurses, psychologists, teachers, spiritual advisors, and countless other people from different walks of life find themselves volunteering for social causes. In these interactions, it is found that the most effective social work response entails a process and an outcome.

From the state's perspective, problems of poverty and housing need political and communal action rather than individual action. Similarly, sexual abuse may be considered a societal issue of male power.

With these examples, you can think of social workers as administrators and policymakers. Unfortunately, you may tend to define social work outcomes in measures that are quantifiable but end up neglecting the subjective accounts (their lived experiences) of the clients.

It is important to remember that an essential aspect of social work is to respond to the emotional needs of the client. They may have difficulties in forming and sustaining relationships, and it is the social worker's responsibility to help them in that struggle. It cannot be downplayed that many problems in society do have origins in societal dynamics (gender inequality, racism, and economics).

For problems that involve mental health, abuse, domestic violence, loss of a beloved, and trauma, it is vital to take into account the disturbances in the emotions and relationships of the clients.

Social therapy, in this regard, is instrumental as it is something that is provided by human influence instead of drugs or technology. These practices may include instruction or objective technique-based approaches.

## Cognitive Behavioral Therapy

Cognitive Behavioral Therapy (CBT) is a model that values the significance of both cognition and behavior, basing the outcomes on behavioral, cognitive, and emotional changes. There are multiple techniques for practicing CBT.

CBT emphasizes the fact that the cause for distress to the client is not the situation itself but how they perceive or interpret it. It aims to readjust the client's frame of thought, promoting the view that emotions, ideas, and behaviors are all interconnected and affect each other.

CBT empowers the client to challenge negative thoughts and bring about change in behaviors that might be considered damaging. For instance, "Automatic Thought Record" is an activity that aims to make the client more self-aware with regards to their thoughts. This self-awareness helps them understand themselves and bring about any necessary changes.

## Crisis Intervention Model

The Crisis Intervention Model aims to support and guide clients suffering from acute mental health crises. These crises are often onset due to Post-Traumatic Stress Disorder (from long term trauma) or recent traumas, and it helps with trauma recovery.

The model plays an instrumental role in helping individuals who are mentally vulnerable enough to cause themselves or others around them, physical harm. The Crisis Intervention Model requires empathetic listening and on-toe analysis of social situations to fix psychosocial problems, making social workers indispensable agents in this model.

The techniques employed while applying this model by the social worker can have a considerable impact on the life of their client. Of the many techniques, the Seven-Stage Crisis Intervention Model is the most reputable. These stages, developed by Roberts and Ottens, aim to set out a logical progression of guidance that helps the social worker in the face of a situation requiring quick decision making.

The steps are:

(1) Conducting a thorough imminent danger assessment.
(2) Establish psychological contact.

(3) Identifying Crisis Precipitants.
(4) Facilitating Emotional Exploration of the Client.
(5) Helping them find Coping Strategies and Alternatives.
(6) Ensuring restoration of functioning through an action plan.
(7) Following up through frequent Booster Sessions.

## Narrative Therapy

Narrative therapy is considered a client-centered and strength-based approach. It is collaborative work between workers and clients that aims to breakdown and question narratives that end up dominating the clients' lives.

Social workers, as narrative therapists, collaborate with clients to make sense of their life's experiences and events. Doing this through a story-telling process that values the different experiences a client may be going through. Then, together, the worker and the client discuss other possible stories, helping helps the social worker in identifying the client's preferred stories. By identifying these, the social worker can then help the client develop a plan for the future.

Narrative therapy interventions rely on externalizing the problem. The externalization process involves redefining problems as external entities – this separates the client from the problem, which grants the client more power and control over their problems. It is a powerful process that relies entirely on the worker's language and metaphorical use, because it plays cultural practices of objectification against itself. In the words of Michael White, "the problem itself is externalized so that the person is not the problem. Instead, the problem is the problem."

Furthermore, narrative therapy may personify problems by asking clients to address the target problem as a roommate or any problematic person with whom they reside. For instance, a client expressing depression could label their depression with a name that is causing them stress or anxiety. Using the roommate metaphor and giving it a name, a social worker can help the client see the external nature of the problem. Instead of asking how long the client has been depressed, you could ask how long their roommate, "X," has resided with them and what's stopping them from kicking them out of their room?

## Solution Focused Therapy

Solution-Focused Therapy (SFT), also known as "Solution-Oriented Therapy," is a short-term model. It is also strength-oriented and aims to identify and enhance the resources available to a client in coping with the problems and difficulties in their life.

The field of family therapy gave way to solution-focused therapy, although many social workers played essential roles in its development. This model tries to alter the pattern that surrounds a problem instead of trying to find root causes – the emphasis is on solutions to the problem instead of the problem itself. SFT practitioners believe that clients have the resources and resolve to solve their problems and that their job is only to help them uncover and activate them.

Techniques like exception-finding (for low problem severity), scaling questions (formulating behavior-specific goals), miracle question (mind development-related), and relationship questions (making the client see themselves from another person's perspective), are used in SFT.

## Task-Centered Practice

Task-centered practice (TCP), in social work, is a model that fosters client-worker collaboration on measurable, specific, and attainable objectives. It is meant to be concise (lasting around 8-12 sessions) and can be used with families, couples, groups, and individuals – making it useful for a wide array of contexts. There are over 40 years of research that backs up TCP's effectiveness, and it is considered one of the social work discipline's oldest "evidence-based practices."

In recent times, due to its versatility, TCP has been incorporated into a wide variety of brief social work models. Generally, it involves a 4-step training process for social workers to work with clients to develop achievable objectives based on the defined problem. The social worker and client identify the problem, the tasks required to address it, and the goals of the treatment.

Throughout the process, TCP gives importance to the preferences of the clients. It instructs workers to ask clients what they want the most to work while they address their problems. Therefore, client strengths and priorities are the cornerstones of the TCP process.

TCP and its phases are versatile, and this enables them to be employed in multiple contexts. The first phase is to successfully define the target problem and establish goals to help deal with it. Phase two involves an agreement by the client and social worker, which also includes a schedule for the changes to be made to resolve the problem. Following several sessions, the third phase begins. Phase three focuses on the level of accomplishment of the goals and if a new TCP process is needed.

While TCP appears to have sequential phases, experts suggest that these phases may overlap, and practitioners need to be well-trained to maximize the benefit of each stage.

# Chapter 15: Social Work as an International Profession

With a globalized world and diminishing borders, social work has also grown to be a truly global profession. International social work aims to promote the practice and education on a worldwide scale, fitting in line with the discipline's goals to respond appropriately and effectively to the ever-evolving global challenges that may significantly impact the world's population.

## Globalization and the International Profession

Globalization is the international integration of all processes related to economic production, distribution, and consumption. Historically speaking, the process started as early as the period of Enlightenment in Europe, and manifests in the market and free-trade principles in the economic theories of Adam Smith, David Ricardio, and modern economists. The WTO, NAFTA, economic aspects of the EU, the World Bank, and IMF are examples of transnational economic processes.

In terms of social work, this means global integration of diverse people, economies, cultures, and political processes without one dominating the others. Globalization implies the emergence of a common international culture, which also includes a shared global awareness. Proof that social work is an international profession.

As an international profession, social work is based on an integrated-perspectives approach that aims to combine human rights, ecological, and other social development perspectives in response to international problems. Because of the global North-South divide, there is an ever-present danger of the Global North imposing on the Global South.

As social workers, it is vital to accept diversity throughout the discipline and a consensus on the overall nature of work. Major emphasis is laid on engagement (i.e., engaging in response to significant global challenges). Most importantly, this response should be driven by a concern for the collective as well as individual wellbeing.

The international social worker must reflect the core values of the profession in all of their practices. Furthermore, they must take action in ensuring uniformity in social work education on the global level and strive for the integration of diverse practices.

It is essential to appreciate the highly interactive nature of this discipline with other fields. For instance, the areas of poverty, ecological destruction, and conflict are often closely related. In terms of cause and effect, poverty and conflict can lead to environmental degradation. Therefore, as social workers, a subjective understanding of the cultures and lives of different populations is crucial.

Finally, there are three general levels of response to global issues; international, national, and local. For instance, for some developmental problems, there could be a response from the United Nations (International), the European Union (regional), or national governments (local). As an international profession, social work covers all of these fields of activity virtually, as long as the international community is involved.

Let us look at some critical International Social Work Organizations and their roles.

## International Federation of Red Cross and Red Crescent Societies (IFRC)

All over the world, there are thousands of volunteers working in communities for the promotion of health, prevention of diseases, and demonstration of positive values vis-à-vis their actions. The IFRC and its National Societies support communities by providing their network of experienced volunteers who practice community-based approaches during their interaction with the community.

The past decade has witnessed significant improvements in global health. Fewer people are dying of measles or malaria, and the number of HIV-infections has reduced in many countries. But the implementation of primary healthcare at the community level has remained a challenge. Statistics that support this include the fact that worldwide, an estimated 14 million people continue dying from infectious diseases. A billion people still don't have access to clean water. Over 500,000 women die due to maternal mortality, and 2.6 billion people lack access to basic sanitation.

The IFRC is a social work organization that addresses health and social services from three dimensions. Firstly, it aims to expand access to primary and public health services for people in underprivileged communities, secondly, to improve health care, and thirdly, to encourage constructive action on the social, behavioral, and environmental aspects associated with good health.

In the discipline of social work, the IFRC has continued work towards the integration of a community-oriented health program instead of disease-oriented initiatives, thus protecting communities from public health crises. The IFRC has maintained an accommodating capacity to head and manage primary international relief operations in spheres of emergency health, sanitation, and access to water.

As a social work organization, it has also advocated and supported advocacy on critical humanitarian issues. It strives to promote human dignity in the war against intolerance, discrimination, and taboos. The IFRC also collaborates with other partners (at the macro and mezzo level) to improve health, economic and social conditions.

In the discipline of social work, the IFRC's partnerships and alliances are a great example of international integration and collaboration. These collaborations are vital to address complex global health challenges brought about by humanitarian crises. The IFRC partnered with WHO and other organizations (active in the health domain) to address these challenges. Besides, it works in global and operational alliances that allow partners to combine their resources to achieve results impossible to attain singlehandedly.

Some examples of the IFRC's partnerships include the Global Water and Sanitation Initiative, the Global Measles Initiative, the Global Polio Eradication Initiative, the chair of the Alliance for Malaria Prevention, the Stop TB Partnership, the Global Network of People Living with HIV, and the UN System Inter-agency Technical Working Group on Influenza.

## IFSW (International Federation of Social Workers)

The IFSW, a part of the three leading international social work organizations, was founded in the late 1920s. The IFSW started as the International Permanent Secretariat of Social Workers (IPSW) in Paris in 1928. It was started by social workers from multiple European countries and the United States. The IPSW dissolved during WWII but was reestablished in the 1950s, and then renamed to the IFSW in 1956.

The fundamental objective of the IFSW was the promotion of social work as a profession with standards and a code of ethics. An International Code Ethics was formulated and adopted in 1976 but was revised later. A secondary goal of the IFSW was to facilitate a global exchange of social workers, made possible through regular conferences. Furthermore, in recent times, the IFSW has been a representative authority on the social work discipline's views on critical world issues. They have published papers in this regard and enjoy a consultative position with the United Nations.

## WHO

Founded in 1948, the World Health Organization (WHO) had a constitution that set its objective as the "attainment by all peoples of the highest possible level of health." It assists global governments (national and international level) to improve their health services, set better healthcare standards, and formulate healthcare regulations and policies. There were 22 functions defined in its constitution that described its role as an indispensable social work organization.

# The Beliefs of International Social Work Practice

After establishing social work as truly an international discipline, it would be appropriate to define the fundamental beliefs and values of international social work.

Interconnectedness: Social, political, and economic events that happen in any part of the world have a direct and immediate impact on the quality of life and human rights around the globe.

Social, Political, and Economic Roots: It is believed that all underlying dynamics of human deprivation and social injustice root from social, political, and economic forces.

Global North-South Divide: International social forces contribute and sustain social inequalities – issues like global poverty and discrimination have substantial international dimensions.

Faith in Peace: Only under peaceful global co-existence and peace can true local, national, and international social development come about.

# Goals of International Social Work

The goals of international social work revolve around enhancing global development and community support.

Eliminating Barriers: To remove impediments to developments such as systemic oppression, which has been used against historically disadvantaged population groups such as women, the aged, children, the disabled, economic and political refugees, the mentally challenged, and other minorities.

Balanced Approach: To realize that a more balanced approach to social and economic development is needed.

Right Priorities: It is vital to ensure that the world gives top priority to human development over other selfish interests.

Expanding Social Work Networks: To mobilize as many people as possible as social workers to help communities get through hardships and support one another.

Poverty Elimination: To eliminate poverty everywhere in the world

Rights for All: The promotion and protection of human rights for all humans

Novel Social Arrangements: To realize that new social arrangements that accelerate the pace of development of humankind.

Promoting Humanity: Incorporating more humane and compassionate values amongst the global society for a more caring world.

# Test 1: Questions

(1) Which of the following best describes the core value of integrity in a social worker?

(A) Must facilitate every individual in need, regardless of differences that co-exist.

(B) Should be able to advocate for the suppressed in society and raise mental health awareness.

(C) Must be trustworthy enough to contribute towards healthy relationships while improving human lives.

(D) Must be skilled in their chosen aspect of social activism.

(2) What qualification are you required to attain to be a licensed social worker in the chosen field?

(A) Undergraduate or postgraduate degrees.

(B) Relevant corporate experience.

(C) Social working experience.

(D) Master of your skills.

(3) What are the three distinct levels of social work practice widely recognized today?

(A) Level 1, level 2, and level 3.

(B) Beginner level, intermediate level, and expert level.

(C) Micro-level, mezzo level, and macro level.

(D) Compassion, social justice, and integrity.

(4) What level of social activism is required in direct interaction and client engagement when addressing personal/interpersonal issues?

(A) Intermediate level.

(B) Integrity.

(C) Level 2.

(D) Micro-Level.

(5) What services should a social worker provide while being on the first level of social activism?

(A) Individual counseling, housing facilitation for the homeless, substance abuse rehabilitation.

(B) Group counseling, advocating for human rights within the community, substance abuse rehabilitation.

(C) Advocating for human rights within the community, individual counseling, campaigning on behalf of the government.

(D) Voluntary healthcare services, group counseling, substance abuse rehabilitation.

(6) What are some of the distinct target clients for the second level of social work?

(A) Groups, families, and government officials.

(B) Healthcare officials, schools, and individuals.

(C) Individuals, families, and schools.

(D) Groups, local organizations, and communities.

(7) Which level of social work is part of organizing of nation-wide activist campaigns?

(A) Level 2 of social work.

(B) The intermediate level of social work.

(C) The expert level of social work.

(D) Macro-level Social Work.


(8) Social workers supporting refugee communities, campaigning for educational rights, and the development of neighborhoods are all segments of a particular level in social activism. Identify the correct level.

(A) Level 3.

(B) Intermediate level.

(C) Mezzo Level.

(D) Social justice level.


(9) Fact Check: Social workers could be involved in more than one of the levels other than the one in which they specialize.

(A) No.

(B) Yes.

(C) Only if they possess a postgraduate degree.

(D) Only if they are certified.

(10)  Why must all social workers understand every level of social work?

(A) To be labeled as a 'professional activist.'

(B) To comprehend and address situations from multiple perspectives.

(C) It is not necessary to understand every level of social work.

(D) To provide better counseling services.


(11)  What is a prominent feature of a successful social worker?

(A) Seamlessly working through, identifying, and incorporating all levels of social work.

(B) It is being able to provide voluntary services without expecting any financial incentive in return.

(C) To be the most qualified academically.

(D) To provide expert level services to local communities.


(12)  Alice is a social activist that provides counseling to individuals who are victims of substance abuse. She then decides to campaign against substance abuse on a national level. What has Alice managed to achieve?

(A) Lower rates of substance abuse, and widespread involvement of similar organizations.

(B) Recognition by the government for her services.

(C) Countrywide awareness of substance abuse.

(D) She managed to work between and across the levels seamlessly.

(13)    Working on a high-level societal system affects which of the following?

(A) Healthcare systems, countries, and individuals.

(B) Individuals, families, and groups.

(C) Entire communities, cities, and countries.

(D) Groups, local organizations, and schools.


(14)    What best describes competence?

(A) Selfless service.

(B) Expanding knowledge to be more skillful and contribute without misrepresentation to clients.

(C) Signifying human relationships and resolving issues to strengthen ties amongst communities.

(D) Working with equality and without classification of any human differences.


(15)    To serve everyone who is in need, globally, to which organizations should social workers be involved?

(A) Public and private charity organizations.

(B) Private charity organizations.

(C) Public charity organizations.

(D) None of the above.

(16) What is the basic foundation on which the field of social work is based?

(A) Social Workers.

(B) Service.

(C) Empathy.

(D) Social Values.

(17) What should a social worker do if the usual services are not meeting the needs of the client?

(A) Continue to provide better service.

(B) Terminate their services.

(C) Refer to a professional.

(D) Ask a colleague for help.

(18) Based on what conditions related to the client, should a social worker not terminate his or her services abruptly?

(A) Client's inability to pay for the services.

(B) Client's misbehavior with the worker.

(C) Services are no longer required.

(D) Financial, social, and romantic interest with the client

(19)   Which values should a social work draw on to help address social issues and help out those who are affected by them?

(A) Knowledge, experience, skills, and values.

(B) Skills, motivation, ethics, and values.

(C) Instincts, professionalism, availability, and skills.

(D) Feelings, skills, values, and experience


(20)   What is the word 'Altruism' used to describe?

(A) The concept of being kind to others.

(B) The ethical doctrine of having a moral obligation to devote oneself to the service of others.

(C) The concept of being selfless.

(D) The concept of social services.


(21)   What should be the primary focus of altruistic help?

(A) Helping those who ask for help.

(B) Expect gratitude for your help.

(C) To help those who will help back.

(D) Relieve the distress of people without receiving anything in return.

(22)  According to evolutionary scientists, what traits can help ensure our survival as a species?

(A) By technological advancement.

(B) Through mutual interests.

(C) Cooperation and help amongst each other.

(D) Being headstrong and ruthless.


(23)  By what is the process through which social workers solve problems between the clients and the community known?

(A) Cooperation.

(B) Social justice.

(C) Egalitarianism.

(D) Morality.


(24)  How can social workers treat their clients with dignity?

(A) By helping them financially.

(B) By being respectful of their differences.

(C) By teaching them ethical values.

(D) By providing them with services.

(25)  What is an essential principle of social work?

(A) Worth.

(B) Social Justice.

(C) Objectivity.

(D) Financial independence.


(26)  By what term is the situation of clients projecting their feelings from personal experiences to their clinicians known?

(A) Communication.

(B) Countertransference.

(C) Inclusivity.

(D) Transference.


(27)  If a social worker feels sympathy towards a client who has been abused in his childhood. What is this reaction of the social worker called?

(A) Countertransference.

(B) Empathy.

(C) Compassion.

(D) Receptiveness.

(28)   What situation can lead to it being challenging to achieve inclusivity in the workplace?

(A)A large number of employees.

(B)Diverse cultural backgrounds.

(C)Norm entrepreneurs.

(D)The nature of the work.


(29)   What value gives a person the ability to do well for himself and bring about positive change to the society?

(A)Dignity.

(B)Worth

(C)Energy.

(D)Belief.


(30)   Which Western philosophical movement that engendered notions of relativism, subjectivity, and fostered mass-skepticism?

(A)Renaissance.

(B)Postmodernism.

(C)Utilitarianism.

(D)Deconstructionism.

(31)	Why do some social workers criticize the Postmodernism movement?

(A) It has created distrust between social workers and the people.

(B) It leads to discrimination.

(C) It creates social injustice in society.

(D) It leads to unemployment.

(32)	Which of the following are the symptoms of burnout?

(A) Insomnia, irritability, and depression.

(B) Violence and hyperactivity.

(C) Creativity and the excessive desire to work more.

(D) Improved performance and productivity.

(33)	What are the two main things required to nurture a relationship?

(A) Love and respect.

(B) Time and energy.

(C) Money and time.

(D) Value and attention.

(34)	What should you do in a healthy relationship that allows you to be your authentic self?

(A) To abstain from competing.

(B) To stop cheating.

(C) To give each other time.

(D) To share secrets.

(35)    Which of the following ways allows the relationship to strengthen?

(A) Good connection.

(B) Mutual understanding.

(C) Secrecy.

(D) Open communication.

(36)    What is one of the reasons people in a relationship feel disconnected from their partner?

(A) Because they start neglecting them.

(B) Because there is a third person in their relationship.

(C) Because they stop sharing in their time of stress.

(D) Because they are dishonest.

(37)    Along with sharing your thoughts, what is one other thing that is important for good communication in a healthy relationship?

(A) Behaving appropriately.

(B) Mutual respect.

(C) Listening.

(D) Passing judgment.

(38) According to the concept of mutual respect, what three behaviors weaken a relationship?

(A) Ignorance, violence, and betrayal.

(B) Disrespect, shouting, and taunting.

(C) Jealousy, disappointment, and cheating.

(D) Insulting, belittling, and ridiculing.

(39) How does one overcome disappointment towards friends/partners in a relationship?

(A) By ending the relationship.

(B) By focusing on their positive attributes.

(C) By asking them to work on their negative attributes.

(D) By having no expectations.

(40) In a relationship, one must not solely depend on a partner or friend for which of the following?

(A) To cater to their emotional needs.

(B) To always help them.

(C) To give them financial help.

(D) To make them feel better.

(41) Which of the following actions can help you process the feeling of hurt that you have experienced in a relationship?

(A) Revenge.

(B) Empathy.

(C) Sympathy.

(D) Forgiveness.

(42) What should you be open and honest about with your partner can help in eradicating feelings of frustration and resentment?

(A) Your limitations.

(B) Your past.

(C) Your thoughts.

(D) Your traumas.

(43) Which principle can help you remain honest with your practices and beliefs, and develop a better understanding of the types of clients with which you want to work?

(A) Morals.

(B) Integrity.

(C) Principles.

(D) Righteousness.

(44) By what are qualities such as honesty, uprightness, consistency, and honor described?

(A) Morals.

(B) Social acceptability

(C) Values.

(D) Integrity.

(45) Which of the following statements best describes the quality of ethical behavior in a social worker?

(A) Social workers should inspire other people to become better by imposing their beliefs upon them.

(B) Social workers should follow their predefined codes of morality and ethics and disregard any other opinion.

(C) Social workers should listen to the problem and offer a solution as a standardized service.

(D) Social workers should understand the problem, show empathy, and offer the best possible advice and counseling services to help the client at their own pace gradually.

(46) Upon what are the values and actions distinguished as either good or bad based?

(A) Philosophies.

(B) Morality.

(C) Integrity.

(D) Beliefs.

(47)     Which of the following best defines the basis of morality in social work?

(A)Morality should be based on benefiting society at large irrespective of your own opinions.

(B)There is only one right answer, and everyone should accept it despite having a different point of view.

(C)Your moral behavior should not be based on what society perceives as the right behavior or what is universally accepted.

(D)The moral codes are the same for every social worker, irrespective of the field, or clients with which they.


(48)     What are the predefined set of values that all social workers are obligated to follow?

(A)Principles.

(B)Morals.

(C)Codes.

(D)Social duties.


(49)     What implies that social workers must establish their relationships with their clients as they are without judgment or resentment?

(A)Prejudice.

(B)Open communication.

(C)Acceptance.

(D)Transparency.

(50)   What is the word 'Confidentiality' is best defined as?

(A) Sharing of personal information.

(B) The notion of respecting the privacy of the clients.

(C) Trusting the social workers.

(D) Making clients confide in you.

(51)   Clients have the right to choose their own path. They can make their own decisions without any sort of pressure or force from social workers. Which of the following principles does the above statement describe?

(A) Justice.

(B) Non-judgment behavior.

(C) Beneficence.

(D) Self Determination.


(52)   While establishing relationships with their clients, what trait should social workers not display?

(A) Confidence

(B) Communicative.

(C) Fairness

(D) Bias

(53) Which of the following is an essential factor in maintaining effective communication with clients?

(A) Active Listening.

(B) Empathy.

(C) Professionalism.

(D) Transparency.

(54) By what term do you define a connection in which the social worker is having personal and professional association with a client?

(A) Partnership.

(B) Private Relationship.

(C) Dual Relationship.

(D) Friendship.

(55) What should social workers must establish and maintain to avoid any ethical issues arising from dual relationships?

(A) Distance.

(B) Professional boundaries.

(C) Expertise and skill.

(D) Morals.

(56)  How do you describe receiving or providing unfair or immoral benefits and advantages through a dual relationship?

(A) Utilizing.

(B) Accomplishing.

(C) Give and Take.

(D) Exploiting.


(57)  Which of the following cannot be classified as a dual relationship?

(A) Having the same social circle.

(B) Belonging to the same advocacy group.

(C) Once off meeting at a social event.

(D) An old school friend.


(58)  Which of the following is an ethical issue associated with forming dual relationships?

(A) Unnecessary demands from a social worker.

(B) Pressurizing or forcing clients to act according to the social worker's wishes.

(C) Exploiting clients by illegally demanding money.

(D) All of the above.

(59)   What can help improve the effectiveness of social services and provide new solutions as well as information to improve social practices and distribution of services?

(A) Evaluation.

(B) Rating.

(C) Judging.

(D) Communication.

(60)   Which of the following levels can be used to assess the performance of social services?

(A) Micro.

(B) Mezzo.

(C) Macro.

(D) All of the above.

(61)   Collecting experimental data, setting targets, and checking accuracy to evaluate social conduct falls under which of the following methods?

(A) Management Oriented.

(B) Scientific Model.

(C) Qualitative Analysis.

(D) Client Based.

(62)   What can assess the performance of the organization as a whole for specific evaluation needs?

(A) Institutional Model.

(B) Management-Oriented Model.

(C) Quality-Based Model.

(D) Client Oriented Model.

(63)   Using focus groups, detailed interviews, and conducting extensive research is part of which evaluation method?

(A) Qualitative research based on observation and client understanding.

(B) Qualitative research based on client interactions.

(C) Theoretical research findings.

(D) Past experiences to evaluate.

(64)   What method is used to identify how content your clients are with your social conduct?

(A) Social group method.

(B) Target-oriented approach.

(C) Client-based approach.

(D) Qualitative approach.

(65) The broad discipline of social work is divided into the following three main categories.

(A) Counselling, micro-counseling, and macro-counseling.

(B) Micro, Mezzo, and Macro levels of social work.

(C) Social work, psychology, and social services.

(D) None of the above.

(66) Which is the most common type of social work with a long-standing history?

(A) Micro-social work.

(B) Mezzo-social work.

(C) Macro-social work.

(D) Non-clinical services.

(67) Which type of social work is included in micro-social work for clients who face challenges and need support.

(A) Mezzo.

(B) Clinical.

(C) Non-Clinical.

(D) Both (B) and (C).

(68)   Activities at which level involve macro and mezzo-social work?

(A) Group.

(B) Individual.

(C) Higher.

(D) Lower.


(69)   Which individuals are mostly dealt with in micro-level social work?

(A) Needy.

(B) Financially strained.

(C) Challenged.

(D) Vulnerable.


(70)   With micro-level social work starting at the very bottom level, what do these social workers have?

(A) More vulnerable clients.

(B) Direct interaction with their clients.

(C) Low qualification.

(D) More passion and compassion.

(71)    What skills do some social workers have, making them more suitable to work at the micro-level?

(A) Resources and passion.

(B) Emotional stability and kindness.

(C) Interpersonal skills and passion for improvement.

(D) Professionalism and patience.

(72)    As an essential aspect of micro social work is its ability to take different forms, what qualities should a social worker within this level have?

(A) Emotional and physical well-being.

(B) Creativity and methodology.

(C) Qualification and Training.

(D) Underlying philosophy and perspective.

(73)    Social workers who want to work at the micro-level must have the following clinical skills.

(A) Listening, empathy, mindfulness, and counseling crisis intervention.

(B) Sympathy, kindness, professionalism, and straightforwardness.

(C) Decision making, empathy, professionalism, and management.

(D) None of the above.

(74)   Which of the following is an example of social work at the micro-level?

(A) A military social worker who supports soldiers to deal with PTSD.

(B) A clinical social worker who provides therapeutic support to their clients.

(C) A Medical social worker who works with sick or critically sick patients.

(D) All of the above.


(75)   What kind of services does a school social worker provide?

(A) Financial help to deserving students.

(B) Tutor them for free.

(C) Help resolve problems of students related to anxiety, depression, and harassment.

(D) Help them to fit in.


(76)   What is meant by the term 'norm entrepreneur'?

(A) Someone interested in social services.

(B) Someone who preaches about social work.

(C) Someone who gives monetary funds for social work.

(D) Someone interested in changing the social norms in a society.


(77)   What are norm entrepreneurs dedicated to that govern our society to eradicate social injustice?

(A) Financial conditions and social issues.

(B) Existing laws and values.

(C) Government policies and laws.

(D) Social services and values.

(78)  Which factor is vital in reforming a society?

(A) More people are inclined towards making a change.

(B) Every individual in society plays a role.

(C) Individuals are motivated to bring about positive change.

(D) All of the above.


(79)  Who coined the concept of 'norm entrepreneurs'?

(A) Bill Gates.

(B) Auguste Comte.

(C) Cass Sunstein.

(D) None of the above.


(80)  When generations and societies are eventually reshaped, what is an altruistic society is developed by?

(A) By changing institutions.

(B) By incorporating personal change.

(C) By keeping out of trouble.

(D) By doing social work.


(81)  How do individuals create a social impact?

(A) By displaying positive habits and behavior.

(B) By volunteering for social services.

(C) By fighting against injustice.

(D) None of the above.

(82)   Which of the following things can an individual do to inflict positive change in society?

(A) Listen respectfully to other people's ideas and problems.

(B) Open yourself to differing opinions.

(C) Both (A) and (B).

(D) None of the above.


(83)   Which combination below feeds the status quo?

(A) Pride and inflexibility.

(B) Differences and Rejections.

(C) Injustice and division.

(D) Ignorance and injustice.


(84)   At which level must change begin to reach a global scale?

(A) Mezzo level.

(B) Micro-level.

(C) Social level.

(D) Government level.

(85)   What kind of services do social workers provide at a micro-level to vulnerable people?

(A) Healthcare, mental health services, and therapy.

(B) Financial services.

(C) Emotional support.

(D) None of the above.

(86)   Other than the people in a position of power, what important factor can facilitate significant changes in society?

(A) Powerful organizations.

(B) Personal transformation.

(C) Norm entrepreneurs.

(D) All of the above.

(87)   Who plays a crucial role in helping families, communities, and individuals by bringing about positive differences in their lives?

(A) Social Workers.

(B) Lawyers.

(C) Engineers.

(D) Soldiers.

(88)   Name the missing of the three levels of social work through which the scope of its benefits extends, mezzo, macro, and?

(A) Micron.

(B) Macroscopic.

(C) Micro.

(D) Subatomic.


(89)   Moving your way between the three levels and working simultaneously on them by combining?

(A) One or more

(B) Two or more

(C) Three-Hundred or more

(D) None of the Above.


(90)   When a social worker providing individual assistance to someone with mental illness or psychological issues said to be operating at which level of social work?

(A) Micro.

(B) Macro.

(C) Mezzo.

(D) Macron.

(91)    When the social worker extends their services to an individual client's family (such as family therapy and counseling), the social worker is said to be operating at which level of social work?

(A) Mozzarella.

(B) Mezzo.

(C) Macro.

(D) Micro.

(92)    When a social worker working on mental health patients decides to reach out to the community with a mental health seminar, they are said to be operating at which level of social work.

(A) Microscopic.

(B) Mozzarella.

(C) Macro.

(D) Mezzo.

(93)    Which nature of social work is reflected in collaboration with different professionals working closely to enhance skills, broaden perspectives, and help society?

(A) Intra-disciplinary.

(B) Interdisciplinary.

(C) Parochial.

(D) Limiting.

(94)   Which of the options listed below has a significant influence on the discipline of social work, such as psychology, human functioning, and children studies?

(A) Behavioral Sciences.

(B) STEM subjects.

(C) Business subjects.

(D) Theories.


(95)   What exchange is a vital part of the social worker identity and an aspect of the discipline's interdisciplinary nature of social work?

(A) Gifts.

(B) Ribbons.

(C) Postage Stamps.

(D) Knowledge.


(96)   Name the impact on society that comes from social workers helping those in need and inspiring other people to work together?

(A) Betterment.

(B) Deterioration.

(C) Destruction.

(D) Appraisal.

(97)    Of the options listed below, who are dealt with at the micro and mezzo levels of social work? They are different levels of analysis in the realm of social work.

(A) NGO's and families

(B) Advocacy Networks and families

(C) Law Firms and families

(D) Individuals and families


(98)    Which level of social work deals with society at large? Unlike the Mezzo Level, it deals with the community and focuses on societal problems and solutions.

(A) Macro.

(B) Mezzo.

(C) Micro.

(D) Mozzarella.


(99)    Of the options listed below, what does one call the pitch, which is a naturally flowing and catchy 30-90 second speech in which the social worker describes and how their work can benefit a client?

(A) Doorbell.

(B) Elevator.

(C) Elaborate.

(D) Long.

(100)  At which level of social work is a coffee shop or lunch meeting an excellent way for social workers to interact with their clients casually?

(A) Micro.

(B) Mezzo.

(C) Macro.

(D) Ideal.

(101)  Which form of media is a great way to connect with people all over the world?

(A) Print.

(B) Block-chain.

(C) Deep Web.

(D) Social.

(102)  Which is the most popular professional social network where individuals from different professional backgrounds form connections with one another?

(A) LinkedIn.

(B) WhatsApp.

(C) Twitter.

(D) MySpace.

(103) Which of the options listed below are activities with various organizations to connect different people and work selflessly is an excellent way of showing that you are committed to the wellbeing of others?

(A) Gaming.

(B) Volunteering.

(C) Fishing.

(D) None of the Above.


(104) What do you call events, such as seminars, webinars, and attending alumni conferences where social workers can meet new people and exchange different ideas?

(A) Sporting.

(B) Racing.

(C) Networking.

(D) Sleeping.


(105) Which of the skills listed below is one of the essential traits of a social worker as they reflect their ability to hear their client out?

(A) Listening.

(B) Oratory.

(C) Drifting.

(D) Visual.

(106) What can social workers build by attending social events, the elevator pitch, volunteering, and using social websites such as Facebook?

(A) Furniture.

(B) Stamp Collection.

(C) Networks.

(D) Financial Assets.


(107) Who is known as the father of social conflict theory?

(A) Karl Marx.

(B) Erik Erikson.

(C) Sigmund Freud.

(D) Auguste Comte.


(108) What did Marx name the privileged and capitalist class of the society?

(A) Bourgeoisie.

(B) Proletariat.

(C) Dominants.

(D) None of these.

(109) Which theory is useful for social workers to find out how the power imbalance of society affects the lives of individuals? With the application of this theory in social work, it is possible to help create consensus among different social classes with battling against the causes of dispute.

(A) Development.

(B) Racialization.

(C) Conflict.

(D) Grounded.


(110) What, according to the Marxist theory of conflict, is the working class?

(A) Bourgeoisie.

(B) Dominant.

(C) Middle Class.

(D) Proletariat.


(111) Which is the theory that targets all the concepts that lead to modernization of "primitive" societies? This theory focuses on the joint effort of all social sectors towards community development. Social Workers work to bring together all the economic sectors to interact with each other to achieve the best results for society.

(A) Development Theory.

(B) Conflict Theory.

(C) Racialization Theory.

(D) Grounded Theory.

(112)   According to whom does an individual goes through eight interrelated stages of development throughout his/her life? The theory plays a significant role in social work interventions as it considers all external factors, for instance, family and society, that contribute effects on an individual's personality.

(A) Karl Marx.

(B) Erik Erikson.

(C) Sigmund Freud.

(D) Auguste Comte.


(113)   At what age are individuals involved in the phase of reflection? This reflection may be either positively associated with pride or negatively associated with despair.

(A) At the age of 65 until death.

(B) Between the age of 20 to 30.

(C) In adolescence.

(D) In preschool years.


(114)   What is a major threat to the integration of the society? It can further lead to social marginalization or alienation.

(A) Ethnicity.

(B) Racism.

(C) Inter-community interactions.

(D) Anti-social behavior.

(115) The segregation of African Americans in the pre-American Civil War era subjects to racial discrimination, which led to one of the vast human marginalizations of history. Of which theory is this a practical example?

(A) Development theory.

(B) Racialization theory.

(C) Conflict Theory.

(D) Psychosocial Theory.


(116) What can welfare programs such as scholarship and employment opportunities for social minorities can help prevent?

(A) Ethnic Diversity.

(B) Inter-Cultural Interactions.

(C) Racism and Marginalization.

(D) None of these.


(117) Which theory proposes that theoretical models must be constructed in data and analysis? This theory revolves around the ideas of systematic methods.


(A) Racialization theory.

(B) Grounded theory.

(C) Conflict theory.

(D) Psychosocial theory.

(118) Grounded Theory is constructed based on data and analysis rather than proposing theoretical models. In conjunction with inductive reasoning, on what data is the Grounded Theory based?

(A) Analytical.

(B) Real-time.

(C) Psychosocial.

(D) None of these.

(119) In Grounded Theory, what do we call the process of coding the collected data in a detailed manner?

(A) Bridging.

(B) Macroanalysis.

(C) Microanalysis.

(D) Integration.

(120) Of the options listed below, which theory derives an empirical connection between experiences of individuals (in family life, community) and systemic realities?. It is an essential aspect of social work as it contributes towards targeted intervention, which is far more effective than other methodologies.

(A) Grounded Theory.

(B) Conflict Theory.

(C) Psychosocial Theory.

(D) None of these.

(121)  Grounded theories are utilized in research studies. What do researchers make use of in conjunction with real-time data collection and analysis?

(A) Scientific methods.

(B) Inductive reasoning.

(C) Theoretical models.

(D) Deductive reasoning.


(122)  Under the approach of which theory do social workers help challenged individuals, such as the homeless, elderly, and the disabled, to take advantage of economic opportunities and fit into the social community?

(A) Development Theory.

(B) Conflict Theory.

(C) Psychosocial Theory.

(D) Grounded Theory.


(123)  What is the term used to describe the social exclusion of a group of people and minorities? When excluded, such groups are subjected to deprivation of fundamental human rights, resources, and opportunities.

(A) Racism.

(B) Marginalization.

(C) Ethnic Conflict.

(D) None of the above.

(124)   The evolution of an individual's development is based on his/her adaptation of social crises throughout the lifespan.  On which theory is the concept which revolves around the individual's response to the world around him/her based?

(A) Erikson's Psychosocial Theory.

(B) Grounded Theory.

(C) Development Theory.

(D) Conflict Theory.


(125)   Under Erikson's eight stages of development, which tends to appear as a key trait in toddlerhood (early childhood, over 18 months to about three years of age)?

(A) Hope.

(B) Will.

(C) Fidelity.

(D) Purpose.

(126)   From Erikson's Eight Stages of Development, "hope" appears as a key trait in which stage of life?

(A) Adolescence.

(B) Toddlerhood.

(C) Infancy.

(D) Late Adulthood.

(127)  In which stage of life are individuals are more fixated on their careers and families. In this period of life, "care" and "responsibility" appear as the key traits in individuals?

(A) Late Adulthood.

(B) Puberty.

(C) Middle Adulthood.

(D) None of these.

(128)  Individuals start seeking love and companionship in which period of their lives? This is the stage of development when the individual has heightened emotions. If the relationships turn out as failures, the individuals might fall into depression. (Keep in view the Erikson's Eight Stages of Development)

(A) Late Childhood.

(B) Young Adulthood.

(C) Adolescence.

(D) Middle Adulthood.

(129)  In which stage of development do individuals develop the desire to copy people around them?

(A) Young adulthood.

(B) Pre-schooling.

(C) Toddlerhood.

(D) Late Childhood.

(130)   Which theory is a framework that is based on the socio-economic behavior of individuals?

(A) Conflict Theory.

(B) Psychosocial Theory.

(C) Rational Choice Theory.

(D) Racialization Theory.


(131)   Who is the founder of the Rational Choice Theory?

(A) Erik Erikson.

(B) George Homans.

(C) Sigmund Feud.

(D) None of these.

(132)   Social activities of all individuals are rationally motivated. These motivations can be based on monetary terms, profit-making, or loss-evasion. Of which theory is this the concept?

(A) Conflict Theory.

(B) Psychosocial Theory.

(C) Rational Choice Theory.

(D) Racialization Theory.

(133)   What is the process that represents the basic unit of social life as the product of individual actions is known as? The process also forms the basis for the Rational Choice Theory, which states that individual behaviors and economic models are interlinked.

(A) Methodological individualism.

(B) Methodological communism.

(C) Methodological socialism.

(D) None of these.

(134)   According to Rational Choice Theory, upon what is an individual's preference of choice based?

(A) Scientific Methods.

(B) Completeness.

(C) Transitivity.

(D) Either completeness or transitivity.

(135)   Which of the following do you think is based on Rational Choice Theory?

(A) Cognitive Behavioral Therapy.

(B) Narrative Therapy.

(C) Task Centered Practice.

(D) None of these.

(136)  Which theory interlinks social behaviors and economic system behaviors? The theory is based on the fact that motivations influence people's decisions in monetary terms, profit analysis, and cost evasion.

(A) Conflict Theory.

(B) Psychosocial Theory.

(C) Rational Choice Theory.

(D) Racialization Theory.


(137)  What must a social worker do when placed in a hypothetical situation?

(A) There are no theoretical situations when working as a social worker.

(B) Seek help from the solutions proposed in the past.

(C) Ask seniors for assistance in regards to the situation.

(D) Tackle them with a pragmatic approach.

(138)  What is the nature of the choice of models in social activism?

(A) Arbitrary.

(B) Rational.

(C) Decisive.

(D) Indecisive.


(139)  Of the options listed below, which combination essentially entails effective social work response?

(A) More clients and recognition.

(B) Improvement of society and social awareness.

(C) Practical approach and conceptual understanding.

(D) A process and an outcome.

(140) How can poverty and displacement of families be addressed from the perspective of a state?

(A)The state does not respond to such problems.

(B)Political justice and community response.

(C)Individual action.

(D)Creating awareness in schools.

(141) A client that grew up in an unpleasant atmosphere and had a traumatic past of domestic violence should be dealt with separately without taking emotional disturbances into account?

(A)Yes, personal life must not cause interference in any welfare aspect.

(B)It depends on the amount of monetary incentive offered.

(C)No, mental health issues and emotional disturbances must be catered for.

(D)Dealing with domestic violence is not part of social activism.

(142) How is social therapy provided for by activists?

(A)Medication provided by pharmaceutical units.

(B)Counseling through human influence.

(C)Radiation of waves in the nervous system to control emotions using technology.

(D)None of the above.

(143)   What model signifies the importance of readjusting the thought process of a client?

(A) Cognitive-behavioral therapy.

(B) Social therapy.

(C) Mental health counseling.

(D) Crisis counseling.


(144)   What best describes Automatic Thought Record.

(A) To counsel clients with medication.

(B) To raise self-awareness in clients about their thought process.

(C) To keep a track record of a client's thoughts.

(D) To assist clients in speaking about their disturbances in life.


(145)   For the crisis intervention model to be used, from what disorder should clients suffering?

(A) Acute mental health crisis.

(B) Seven-stage crisis.

(C) Post-traumatic events.

(D) Mental disorders.

(146)   A social worker implying the crisis intervention model would initially resort to the most reputable technique. Which of the following is that technique?

(A) Second-stage stress intervention model.

(B) Post-traumatic stress intervention model.

(C) Seven-Stage crisis intervention model.

(D) Self-reflect intervention model.


(147)   Who developed the stages of technique when applying the Crisis Intervention Model?

(A) Richard and Owen.

(B) Robert and Ottens.

(C) Rick and Oberon.

(D) Rett and Otto.


(148)   Of the most reputable technique in Crisis Intervention Model, identify (in order) what step comes after 'Conducting a thorough and imminent danger assessment'?

(A) Inquire about the client's past.

(B) Facilitation of medication.

(C) Identifying crisis precipitants.

(D) Establish psychological contact.

(149)  What best describes 'following up through frequent booster sessions'?

(A) Therapeutic sessions to ensure the sanity and well-being of the client.

(B) Medication-based treatment to ensure the well-being of the client.

(C) The advice was given to a client to engage in healthy physical activity.

(D) The advice was given to a client to attend relevant motivational speaking seminars.


(150)  What is narrative therapy?

(A) When a client listens to impactful narratives shared by similar victims to change their mindset.

(B) Social workers collaborating with clients to establish and look into narratives that influence and impact the client's lives.

(C) Social workers providing regular therapy sessions to clients.

(D) Clients discussing their strengths and weaknesses with the social worker.

# Test 1: Answers & Explanations

(1) (C) Must be trustworthy enough to contribute towards healthy relationships while improving human lives.

Social workers must possess integrity for clients to be comfortable while being under their influence. A credible social worker must be trustworthy enough for individuals to rely upon and for activists to encourage good relationships and strengthen ties. Consistently being able to improve the lives of people is an objective every social worker must bear in mind while achieving the core value of integrity.

(2) (A) Undergraduate or postgraduate degrees.

Most of the social workers tend to gain experience by practically applying their skills in their respective fields. However, before attaining experience, to be a professional/licensed social worker, you must have relevant academic knowledge to cater to theoretical problems with practical solutions.

(3) (C) Micro level, mezzo level, and macro level.

The social work industry allows a diversified employment setting that individuals must cope with to cater to those in need. The complexity and interdisciplinary nature involved is what sets social activism apart from other professions, which is why it is categorized into three different levels to avoid mishandling of any situation. The three levels are micro, mezzo, and macro, all of which are interlinked with one another, and the actions of one level could most definitely impact the others.

(4) (D) Micro Level.

When we think about services provided by a social worker, we most likely refer to an activist working at micro-level dealing with personal and interpersonal scenarios. Micro-level of social work is the most common of the three levels and requires one-to-one handling of the client's issues and direct interaction.

(5) (A) Individual counseling, housing facilitation for the homeless, substance abuse rehabilitation.

Working for the micro-level social activism requires workers to facilitate individuals and families, and resolve matters that exist on a smaller scale. Substance abuse therapy, individual counseling services, rehabilitation sessions, and assisting the homeless, are all efforts made by an activist working on a micro-level.

(6) (D) Groups, local organizations, and communities.

Unlike working at micro levels, the social work that takes place on the secondary level, i.e., Mezzo level, involves social activists to slowly expand their base/level by catering to groups rather than individuals and resolving issues on a slightly larger scale. Groups, schools, local organizations, and communities are all part of the Mezzo level.

(7) (D) Macro-level social work.

Macro-level social work is the most extensive and most expanded base of the three levels of social activism that involves large scale projects. Such projects contribute to cities and even countries. Organizing nationwide campaigns and awareness programs is a segment of social work that falls under the macro level.

(8) (C) Mezzo Level.

The mezzo level is a more comprehensive prospect in social activism that caters to numerous issues that arise within local communities, groups, and local organizations. The involvement of social workers in the mezzo level includes but is not limited to, advocacy work for refugees, educational campaigning, and development of neighborhoods.

(9) (B) Yes.

Social workers are not limited to work in only one of the levels in which they specialize. In most cases, the levels are interlinked, and activists have the option to be occupationally mobile between the levels or even being involved in all three.

(10)    (B) To comprehend and address situations from multiple perspectives.

Regardless of a social worker specializing in a particular level, all workers need to have in-depth knowledge and understanding about the other levels. They must also be able to respond well in situations that call for the incorporation of two or more levels at once to address an issue.

(11)    (A) Seamlessly working through, identifying, and incorporating all levels of social work.

The ability to identify challenges and smoothly work in between all three of the social levels is a critical feature that depicts the success and professionalism of a social worker.

(12)    (D) She managed to work between and across the levels seamlessly.

The hypothetical situation depicts that Alice had been able to work between levels feasibly, and that is made evident by her involvement as a social worker starting from individual counseling to creating nationwide awareness campaigns.

(13)    (C) Entire communities, cities, and countries.

When dealing with issues on a macro level, it involves catering to problems that impact society as a whole. Communities, cities, and even countries all benefit from the social work that is conducted on macro levels.

(14)     (B) Expanding knowledge to be more skillful and contribute without misrepresentation to clients.

Consistently expanding knowledge about the domain, an activist tends to work in to be more successful and professional is what depicts competence. Misrepresentation of one's skills to clients defies the purpose of remaining competent.

(15)     (A) Public and private charity organizations.

With the advancement of professionalism in social activism, both private and public charitable organizations have played significant roles in conducting and contributing to a better society.

(16)     (B) Services.

Services are a collection of actions that involves helping or doing work for others. Since social work is a field where professionals provide services to those in need, the primary constituent on which social work is based is to provide 'service' to others.

(17)     (C) Refer to a professional.

According to the guidelines provided by the Code of Ethics of the National Association of Social Workers, a social worker must try to make every possible effort to provide their services to the client. However, if they see that their client may require an expert's help, then they are required to refer them to a professional. Also, they should ensure an orderly transfer of responsibility when referred to as an expert.

(18)     (D) financial, social, and romantic interest with the client.

According to the guideline provided by the Code of Ethics of the National Association of Social Workers, a social worker is not allowed to terminate their services based on any type of financial, social, or romantic interest with the client. On the contrary, it is considered incredibly unprofessional to not inform the client before termination or before the transfer of responsibility has been dealt with smoothly.

(19)    (A) Knowledge, experience, skills, and values.

As a social worker, one must contribute towards addressing social problems and putting others' needs before their own. Thus, this requires social workers to depend heavily on their knowledge of social problems and how to address them skillfully. They also require experience, values, and a set of great skill so that they can work on behalf of their clients who cannot do it themselves.

(20)    (B) The ethical doctrine of having a moral obligation to devote oneself to the service of others.

The word altruism originated from Latin and was used by a French Philosopher, Auguste Comte, in the 19th century. He used the word to describe selflessness and concern for the happiness of others, including renouncing one's self-interests and personal agendas.

(21)    (D) Relieving the distress of people without receiving anything in return.

The meaning of altruism is to promote the welfare of others without thinking about your gains. Altruistic help is voluntary, and the helper does not demand any sort of reward, gratitude, or repayment in return.

(22)    (C) Cooperation and help amongst each other.

According to revolutionary scientists, there are deep-rooted altruistic traits present in human beings. Much evidence backs the fact that to cooperate rather than compete is one of the people's first impulses.

(23)    (C) Egalitarianism.

The concept of egalitarianism is to resolve all conflicts of interest between clients and the broader society. It builds on the doctrine of social justice and ensures that all members of society are treated with equality. The knowledge generally categorizes egalitarian principles that all humans are equal in essential worth or moral status and must be treated as such.

(24)    (B) By being respectful of their differences.

To treat everyone with dignity, social workers need to learn to be mindful of individual differences such as idiosyncrasies and personal faith, as well as culture and ethnicity. They should ensure that no person is discriminated against or alienated and that their behavior with all clients is the same. They should be respectful towards the beliefs, cultures, values, and norms of all of their clients.

(25)    (B) Social Justice.

Social justice principles are those values that facilitate the goal of reducing inequalities, promoting diversity, and uplifting the vulnerable segments of society. It is an essential component of social work. It requires that all members of society must be treated with equity and respect. No group should be marginalized, and equal opportunities of progress should be presented to everyone.

(26)    (D) Transference.

Transference occurs when a client redirects or projects their feelings from an important person in their life (a significant other or a close relation) to the clinician. It most often occurs in a therapeutic setting where clients reveal their past traumas to their therapists and expose them towards traumatic feelings that they can carry into their lives unconsciously. It can have both positive and negative impacts on the social worker.

(27)    (A) Countertransference.

Countertransference is a psychological concept that redirects a psychotherapist's emotion towards a client. It is a natural reaction to transference. It may cause the therapist to react unfavorably in response to their client's transference as they may carry their impacts in their personal lives.

(28)　(B) Diverse cultural backgrounds.

Inclusivity is the practice of including all people without discriminating against or alienating any person. It can be challenging to achieve due to social workers hailing from different socio-economic and socio-cultural backgrounds. An inclusive work environment consists of a diverse workforce with people from all walks of life working together towards a common goal.

(29)　(B) Worth.

An individual's worth can be defined as the conviction in the capacity they have to improve the lives of themselves and those around them. A person can cater to his own needs and be a valuable member of society. It is the self-perceived value of an individual. One of the goals of social workers is to make their clients realize their worth and how they are capable of changing their situation themselves.

(30)　(B) Postmodernism.

The postmodernism movement started in the 1980s and led to a significant change in Western societal philosophies. It included the person-in-environment concept, which was associated with social work practice. It also led to mass skepticism against the profession due to its subjectivity.

(31)　(A) It has created distrust between social workers and the people.

Some social workers criticized the postmodernism movement because it was attributed to the enormous trust deficit between the masses and the social workers. People began viewing social work as a "subjective effort" for a "subjective cause," leading to a decline in the quality of social work globally.

(32)   (A) Insomnia, irritability, and depression.

Burnouts can also lead to depression, which can cause a lack of enthusiasm for activities the social worker may have once enjoyed. They could display symptoms of insomnia and a lack of patience with their clients and may be continuously distracted by intrusive thoughts. Owing to the uncertain and tolling nature of social work, they inevitably end up with sleep-disturbance and insomnia – these are dangerous symptoms of burnout as it affects their overall performance and can lead to irritability.


(33)   (B) Time and energy.

Relationships are fragile, but they can be made secure by putting much effort into them. Effort requires time, and every relationship needs to pass a threshold to make it through. They require empathy, commitment, and excellent communication, and this needs energy.


(34)   (A) to abstain from competing.

When a person stops competing and comparing with the other person, the relationship eventually strengthens. This healthiness in a relationship allows you to feel safe enough to be yourself.


(35)   (D) Open communication.

Open communication is essential because it brings friendliness between two people. They trust each other more and discuss their affairs. With this trust, the relationship nourishes.


(36)   (C) Because they stop sharing in their time of stress.

People in a relationship feel close to one another when there is trust, and this happens when they share their problems, thoughts, and become vulnerable to each other.

(37)    (C) Listening.

For a successful relationship, people must listen to each other attentively without jumping to conclusions. If you want to have excellent communication in a relationship, then you must be fully present so that the other person is willing to share their feelings.

(38)    (D) Insulting, belittling and ridiculing.

Even though countless negative emotions can weaken a relationship, but when people don't respect each other in a relationship, things such as insulting and derogatory remarks become the reason for this to weaken.

(39)    (B) By focusing on their positive attributes.

Disappointments are a part of every relationship, but the key is not to dwell in them but to overcome them. Unrealistic expectations can often lead to disappointment in a relationship. That is why the best way to deal with them is to focus on the expectations your partner/friend has fulfilled.

(40)    (A) To cater to their emotional needs.

It is essential to understand that you should give the other person in the relationship space to avoid conflict. You should not always depend on them for your emotional needs because they might be expecting the same thing in return. There should be a balance in every relationship.

(41)    (D) Forgiveness.

Forgiveness is a potent tool that can help a person move on from other painful feelings. Forgiving doesn't mean that you stop hurting or you have forgotten, but it merely gives the other person a chance to improve or communicate their side. It allows you to process your hurt in the best way possible.

(42)    (A) Your limitations.

Honesty is essential for building trust in a relationship. It is healthy to set boundaries and limitations in a relationship. The most important thing is to be open and honest about those limitations so that the other person understands beforehand.

(43)    (B) Integrity.

Having integrity is an essential part of a social worker. It helps them decide which professional field of social work they want to take on and continue. It also helps them form a special connection with their clients as they can identify themselves with them.

(44)    (D) Integrity.

Showing integrity implies that a person remains honest to their beliefs and principles. Morality defines how a person should behave; whereas, integrity is about your actions during a social activity and how you say consistent.

(45)    (D) Social workers should understand the problem, show empathy, and offer the best possible advice and counseling services to help the client at their own pace gradually.

Being a social worker is not just about following a predefined set of rules and being orthodox. It is about stepping into the shoes of your clients and understanding their point of view. Once you realize what they are going through and how they must be feeling, you will be of better service to them.

(46)    (B) Morality.

Morality teaches you the difference between right and wrong. It guides you to choose the correct thing to do, which would not contradict or negatively impact society. It is a code of conduct that is generally acceptable and is for the wellness of people as well as yourself.

(47)   (A) Morality should be based on benefiting the society at large irrespective of your own opinions.

The morals of people may vary. Some people may accept something as morally correct; whereas, other people may have different views. The important thing is to ensure is that your actions and behavior should be based on benefiting society at large rather than seeking out your interests.

(48)   (A) Principles.

Certain principles are predefined for all social workers. They are a general set of rules that teach you ethical conduct and values. These principles are universally applicable and are accepted by anyone who lives by the laws of morality and correct social conduct.

(49)   (C) Acceptance.

The principles of ethics teach social workers to accept their clients as they are. You must develop a professional relationship with them and never condescend them or show any sort of resentment towards them. You should not expect your clients to be the way you want them to be.

(50)   (B) The notion of respecting the privacy of the clients.

Maintaining confidentiality between social workers and clients is an integral part of social service. There are many things that your clients might tell you in confidence, and it is your moral duty to ensure that it remains between you and the client. Respecting the confidentiality of information is part and parcel of the ethical code of conduct.

(51)   (D) Self Determination.

Your clients have the right to make their own choices. The principle of self-determination teaches you to let the clients have their own free will. They can either follow your advice or choose to do otherwise. As a social worker, you cannot impose your decision on them, and you cannot force them to make decisions that you want them to make.

(52)    (D) Biased.

One of the most important principles of good social conduct is being impartial. Social workers should have a non-judgmental attitude towards their clients. They should not form opinions based on what their clients tell them. Moreover, their conduct should not be influenced by them being biased towards the client's opinions or beliefs.


(53)    (A) Active Listening.

Social workers must have the quality of being a good listener. The key to effective communication is the ability to listen and understand what the other person is saying. Social workers should provide their expert opinion and advice after careful consideration and must pay attention to what their clients have to say.


(54)    (C) Dual Relationship.

A social worker having dual relationships with their clients is not uncommon. It is also one of the reasons why conflicts occur during social work if these relationships are not handled properly. A social worker may be involved with the client on a personal level as an old friend, acquaintance, or family friend.


(55)    (B) Professional boundaries.

Every social worker must know how to maintain professional boundaries with their clients. The social worker should avoid engaging in any sort of irrelevant personal discussions with their clients to ensure that no lines are crossed.


(56)    (D) Exploiting.

One of the repercussions of being involved in a dual relationship with your client is exploitation. Social workers have a higher probability of exploiting their clients and influencing their course of action. Exploitation can take on many forms. For example, a social worker may use their power to change or affect the opinions or beliefs of their clients or vice versa.

(57)    (C) Once off meeting at a social event.

Dual relationships can be formed on various occasions. They are not just limited to sexual partners, family members, or long-term friendships. However, you must not confuse dual relationships with someone you barely even know or have only met once or twice. Your relationship with your clients will not be considered dual until and unless it takes a turn towards a personal level from being professional.

(58)    (D) All of the above.

Dual relationships can put clients in very awkward positions. The social workers exert their powers and force their clients to say or do things they don't want to do. They may provide biased opinions and even try to exploit their clients by striving to seek unnecessary data for their interest.

(59)    (A) Evaluation.

The process of evaluation is part of social work practice as it helps to improve the outcome of the social services being provided. It can help you look at a problem differently and explore more options for solutions. It is a way of assessing yourself and your work to identify any gaps and focus on improvement.

(60)    (D) All of the above.

You can evaluate any of the levels, i.e., micro, mezzo, and macro. The idea behind assessing the performance of social work is to check the effectiveness of social conduct and practices.

(61)    (B) Scientific Model.

The scientific method provides accurate data based on experiments and observation. These experiments are goal-oriented and use relevant information to produce a desirable outcome.

(62)    (B) Management Oriented Model.

This approach acts as a guide to help social workers and organizations plan their operations and identify where any improvements can be made for the betterment of the society at large.


(63)    (A) Qualitative research based on observation and client understanding.

Most of the essential data is recorded and found by observation. Social workers can observe how different clients interpret a similar situation differently; it helps to evaluate your social conduct as well as how effectively you can put your point across to make someone understand.


(64)    (C) Client-based approach.

The client-based or client-oriented approach is used to get an insight into how the clients feel about social activities. They provide their feedback and suggestions, which helps social workers evaluate social activities. This approach focuses on the clients and is effective in getting reliable information as well as providing new solutions.


(65)    (B) Micro, Mezzo, and Macro levels of social work.

Social work is an incredibly broad field that covers activities from one-to-one to higher levels.


(66)    (A) Micro-social work.

This category of social work pertains to one-on-one counseling services for people in need. It has a long-standing history in the professional field that involves working closely with the individual, families, or groups who need support.

(67)    (D) Both (B) and (C).

Micro-social work means working with individuals and families to provide the services and support for the challenges or the injustice they face in the social system. It includes clinical social work that involves dealing with clients in a therapeutic capacity. Moreover, non-clinical services are also included in this category.

(68)    (C) Higher.

Unlike micro-social work, the most common, mezzo and macro social work pertain to social activities at a higher level than micro.

(69)    (D) Vulnerable.

Micro-social work includes social work activities at a very grass-root level. Social workers working on micro-level provide services to the most vulnerable individuals of society, which includes children, disabled people, victims of domestic abuse, and older people.

(70)    (B) Direct interaction with their clients.

Social workers who work at a micro-level deal with the most vulnerable people, and thus dealing with them at a very personal level to provide support. They provide their services at the lowest level to pull individuals out of their sufferings.

(71)    (C) Interpersonal skills and passion for improvement.

People with a passion for improving others' lives and having the power to interact with individuals at a personal level are best suited for social work at a micro-level. This profession is gratifying because people can directly observe their results.

(72)    (D) Underlying philosophy and perspective.

Those dealing with clients on a micro-level include dealing with clients on a personal level. However, it can take different forms as some workers might prefer to solve personal problems while others would want to resolve the social issue that is causing the problem.

(73)    (A) Listening, empathy, mindfulness, and counseling crisis intervention.

Social workers working at a micro-level must have specific skills and knowledge to deal with the issues of their clients. They need to be knowledgeable about the family, group, and interpersonal dynamics.

(74)    (D) All of the above.

Social work at the micro-level has many different forms. It can be anyone from a clinical social worker to a school social worker who provides counseling, guidance, and health care services to those related to that field.

(75)    (C) Help resolve problems of students related to anxiety, depression, and harassment.

School social work is an excellent example of micro-social work. It includes providing support services to students who are victims of depression, anxiety, health problems, harassment, bullying, or other family issues.

(76)    (D) Someone interested in changing the social norms in a society.

Cass Sunstein, in 1996 coined the concept of norm entrepreneurs as a segment of the population that is interested in changing the fragile social conditions and the underlying social system.

(77)    (B) Existing laws and values.

Norm entrepreneurs take it upon themselves to break traditional values and bring forth those norms that are best suited to the needs of every individual. They are dedicated to improving existing laws and values that can result in any form of injustice to the population.

(78)    (D) All of the above.

Societies are reformed when every individual in it plays their part to bring positive change. It is not necessary that only institutions can transform individuals, but individuals can also evolve the institution and eradicate social issues.

(79)    (C) Cass Sunstein.

Cass Sunstein coined the concept in 1996.

(80)    (B) By incorporating personal change.

Before setting out to change society, the first step is to start with yourself. Without how we, as individuals, improve ourselves, society will not reform. What we do now as an individual will affect our children and their children. Therefore, we must start the change with ourselves.

(81)    (A) By displaying positive habits and behavior.

As discussed previously, change starts from an individual first, and then it spreads to the society. Therefore, society is most impacted by displaying individual behavior and practicing positive habits that influence others.

(82)    (C) Both (A) and (B).

One of the best ways to bring about change is to become accepting and tolerant of other people's ideas, values, and problems. We must accept others and understand their perspective rather than forcing or rejecting them. Accepting each other's differences is crucial for resolving social issues.

(83)    (D) Ignorance and injustice.

To beat the status quo, people from all walks of life must come together to fight against injustice and take a stand for vulnerable people. Accepting injustice and ignoring the rights of the weak will strengthen the wheel of cruelty.

(84)    (B) Micro-level.

We all know that a society will only change when it's individuals start to change for good. Impact on a higher level only happens when the seed of change is sown at the grass-root level, and that is the micro-level. Social workers recognize this fact, and that is why they dedicate their efforts in transforming the society.

(85)    (A) Healthcare, mental health services, and therapy.

Micro-level social workers interact with their clients on a personal level. Services such as therapy, healthcare, and emotional support help vulnerable people out of their suffering and issues.

(86)    (B) Personal Transformation.

Even though it would require much time, but individual transformation and personal changes can help facilitate more significant changes in society. People in power aren't the only ones who can bring upon positive changes.

(87)    (A) Social Workers.

As a social worker, it is vital to acknowledge the significance of this profession and how it differs from the rest. Social workers have some key core values that are instilled in them, and they play the crucial role of helping families, facilitating communities, and individuals and bring about positive change, all while contributing towards a healthier and satisfactory environment in which to live.

(88)    (C) Micro.

The role of social workers could be quite similar to one another; however, the employment setting may be very diverse, which could also prove to be advantageous due to the broad scope and perspective the profession has. A social worker could primarily work for one of the three levels being; Micro level, Mezzo Level, and Macro Level. The Micro-level is the grass-root level of social work, which deals with individual connections and issues. The client is always the individual when operating at the micro-level, and therefore, the magnitude of the issues that are expressed are scalable.

(89)    (B) Two or more

While the employment setting of the social worker may be diverse, the existence of levels between the profession of social activism makes it more convenient to scale issues, as per the intensity it holds. A social worker can be able to switch to or work between the three levels of social work, where two or more levels may be worked on simultaneously during the social worker's job. A social worker that was previously committed to working for a small organization or a local neighborhood community against substance abuse and then chooses to advocate for victims nationwide depicts the work setting transitioning from mezzo to macro level.

(90)    (A) Micro.

As the social worker is providing individual assistance in this scenario, it is a case of the Micro Level of social work. The kind of work doesn't matter when you're dealing with levels; all that matters is the nature of the client. Therefore, as per the hypothetical situation, it depicts the nature of the work setting that involves catering to individuals, which is at the entail level of social activism.

(91)    (B) Mezzo.

Mezzo level of social work is the secondary stage to work for in this profession. It involves dealing with issues that are on a slightly larger scale and have more severe impacts relative to the issues handled at the micro-level. For instance, A social worker that may have initially just dealt with an individual's mental health issues, when they begin dealing with their family's problems as well, they operate at the Mezzo Level. Remember, the Mezzo level of social work deals specifically with the family level.

(92)    (C) Macro.

Macro-level social workers work at the community and systems-level. In contrast, mezzo-level social work focuses on neighborhoods, families, small groups, and institutions, which is a level that lies between the two ends of the spectrum. Micro-level work focuses on individuals mainly and is the most common out of all the levels when most of us tend to imagine the job description of a social worker; we are most likely referring to activist groups and individuals working for the micro-level. Micro-level targets smaller issues and involves a one-to-one dialect in an attempt to resolve the issue, whereas the other two levels require a lot more than that. As the level goes higher, so does the magnitude of the problem, and countermeasures taken.

(93)    (B) Interdisciplinary.

Social work involves professionals from diverse backgrounds coming together to solve societal problems selflessly, making it a discipline of collaboration with an interdisciplinary nature. Knowledge and skills are put to the test and are used collectively in addition to diverse professions being incorporated with different areas of social work. The interdisciplinary nature results in collaboration and an attempt to work closely and gain a broader perspective of the work setting while also enhancing skills.

(94)    (A) Behavioral Sciences.

Behavioral Sciences deal with the behavioral aspects of humans. Psychology, human functioning, and the study of children are all examples of behavioral sciences.

(95)    (D) Knowledge.

Social workers hail from different professional backgrounds. It not only makes this interdisciplinary, but the exchange of knowledge plays a vital role in the social worker identity. Regardless, of the social workers academic or professional background, from an activist's point of view, making the most of life and work experiences while learning from your strengths and weaknesses and contributing to being a dedicated social worker that is committed to delivering the best for others, selflessly.

(96)    (A) Betterment.

The fundamental teaching of social work, as a discipline, to its followers (the social workers), is to strive to improve the condition (betterment) of society. It is the main objective that almost every social worker has in mind and is a goal that most want to achieve. Working rigorously for society and prioritizing other's needs before your own is a trait that every social worker must possess. Working and improving societies for the better, creating a positive difference, is what should matter to a social worker in exchange for their selfless services.

(97)    (D) Individuals and families

The Micro level of social work deals exclusively at the grass-root level (that is at the individual level), this involves catering to minor issues that stem from problems that may arise within people's minds. Therapy, counseling, and other similar sessions that consist of a worker-client environment and interaction calls for micro-level of social work—the mezzo level deals with issues at a relatively larger scale, including small groups and families.

(98)   (A) Macro.

The Macro Level of Social work deals with the greater society and community. Macro-level social workers work at the community and systems-level, whereas mezzo-level social work focuses on neighborhoods, small groups, and institutions. Micro-level is a more modest level of social activism. This level of work focuses on families or individuals and could be a result of an issue that may have initially existed in an individual and had then turned out to have adverse impacts over the other family members or neighbors. Though both may be closely related, especially the transitioning between the two, the employment setting is still quite distinct, and the work tends to differ.

(99)   (B) Elevator.

The elevator pitch is a 30 to 90 seconds speech in which you describe yourself and talk about what you do and how you can benefit the other person. An elevator speech should have a natural flow to catch the attention and interest of the other person. You can talk about your goals and what you wish to accomplish in life to leave a positive legacy. It creates a first impression, and therefore, must be very interactive and engaging for the message that you are trying to convey (that means subliminal) to seep into the minds of the audience or the individual that you are targeting. It is an excellent way of networking and being social overall. The elevator pitch is a concise time frame of speech that could leave a very significant impact on somebody's life, so choose your words wisely.

(100)   (A) Micro.

Micro-Level tasks are all about catering to clients on a smaller scale; this involves dealing with problems that are limited to an individual or a family at maximum. Social workers try various methods to engage with such clients to build a relationship of trust and compassion, just as long as they can achieve their goal, i.e., to respond to and address a client's problems swiftly. Under the hypothetical circumstance given above, it depicts an informal client-worker meeting, and using such tactics for interaction usually makes the other person feel more comfortable while talking. It works on a micro-level as it makes the client feel like they can connect better.

(101)   (D) Social.

The benefits that social media has to offer are innumerable; therefore, it is not surprising to know of the many impacts social media has had over the field of activism and how it has managed to change the dynamics for the better. Social media offers contemporary social workers a great avenue to connect with people all over the world (clients and peers alike). This form of networking is preferred by most social workers working at almost every kind of level. Engaging with new clients, virtually being able to reach out to those who need assistance, connecting with similar humanitarian-based individuals and organizations, frequent follow-up sessions to ensure sanity of a client are some of the tasks that could be performed with the help of social media.

(102)   (A) LinkedIn.

LinkedIn is a professional social media website that let's social workers connect with like-minded professionals and organizations that share their vision of societal upheaval.

(103)   (B) Volunteering.

Nothing shows how committed a social worker is to the wellbeing of others more than engaging in volunteering activities, and various organizations allow and provide them with such opportunities. Volunteering opportunities by renowned organizations for individuals who are new to the field of social activism, enables such workers to expand their knowledge, enhance their skills while practically putting them to the test, increasing work experience, and work in different employment environments. Core values are instilled with the practice of volunteering as individuals may work selflessly without having expectations for a monetary incentive in exchange for the services that they may be providing.

(104)   (C) Networking.

There are various seminars and webinars for social workers to attend where they can meet new people and exchange ideas – this is called networking.

(105) (A) Listening.

In the field of social activism, it is vital to have some key traits to qualify as an exceptional social worker. Listening skills are one of the essential characteristics of a social worker. It enables them to hear the client's story, deduce problems, and advise solutions. While a worker may be interacting with the client, it is vital that the worker carefully listens to all the details of the client's narratives, instead of interrupting and proposing potential solutions without acknowledging the root of the problem or taking the client's emotional state of mind into consideration. A social worker must also identify their (the client's) strengths and weaknesses and analyze their priorities and inclinations; this allows the worker to ultimately form solutions or plot possible ways to counter the issues with which the client is dealing.

(106) (C) Networks.

Working as a social worker requires the effort to consistently expand one's network to reach a larger audience and also find potential organizations to collaborate with, which could involve the benefit of both. Attending social events (such as webinars and seminars), elevator pitching, using social media forums, and meeting up with clients at a coffee shop – all of these help to build networks. Regardless of the level, a social worker may be working on; it may be relevant at one point or another to connect and expand services provided on a broader scale, this is especially important for workers working in between two or more levels.

(107) (A) Karl Marx.

Karl Marx created the social conflict theory. He primarily focused on the cause of the effect of class differences. He studied the conflict between the bourgeoisie-the capitalists and the proletariat-the working-class intensely and was of the viewpoint that this conflict could provoke social change in society.

(108) (A) Bourgeoisie.

Marx coined the term "bourgeoisie" for the economic ruling social class. This class belonged to those who owned the society's land and capital (i.e., the means of production).

(109)   (C) Conflict.

The social conflict theory constructed by Karl Marx is the primary paradigm of sociology, while at the same time contributes to being a significant part of social work. To depict how societal conflicts influence an individual's life to prove helpful to create plans of how to try overcoming such differences. The conflict theory, in short, helps social workers in client assessment and mediation strategy.

(110)   (D) Proletariat.

Marxist theory of conflict terms the oppressed working class of the society as the Proletariats. This class struggles against the social instability imposed by the economic ruling class, also known as the bourgeoisie (the capitalists), according to Marx.

(111)   (A) Development theory.

Development Theory is the collection of ideas on how societies can move towards a positive change. Social workers incorporate the Development theory along with concepts of modernization to help move the society towards development.

(112)   (B) Erik Erikson.

Erik Erikson was a German psychoanalyst who gave the psychosocial theory of development. According to Erikson's theory, an individual undergoes eight stages of development in his/her lifespan, and further revolves around multiple aspects of identity. These include the ego, personality, and the social identities of an individual. The eight stages of development include infancy, early childhood years, preschool age, school attending age, adolescence, young adults, middle-aged adults, and late adults. The theory helps social workers widely in client assessment and intervention strategy.

(113)    (A) At the age of 65 till death.

Late adults, mostly over the age of 65 years till death, reflect widely on their lives. Those who have led a meaningful life look back at their lives with happiness and relief. On the contrary, those who had to go through failures are subject to despair and disappointment. In short, Erikson's stage of development is related to human self-reflection.

(114)    (B) Racism.

Racial discrimination is a significant obstacle in the way of achieving integration among a community. Physical differences between cultures, such as eye color, skin color, height, facial features, and hair color, are subject to racial discrimination. This sort of discrimination can further lead to marginalization, i.e., social segregation of minorities.

(115)    (B) Racialization theory.

Racialization Theory suggests that depriving a community of its fundamental human rights, based on racial discrimination, can lead to human marginalization. The same happened to the African Americans based on their skin color. They were subjected to segregation that later followed by marginalization.

(116)    (C) Racism and Marginalization.

Racism and Marginalization have a strong association with one another. The consequences of the segregation of a group can never be favorable for societal development. History is evident that whenever social discrimination prevailed, society had to deal with social instability followed by protests and retaliation to bring about change in the existing system. However, introducing such welfare programs can help restore social integration and cohesion. It is an effective method to eradicate any sort of discrimination that might be present and to set forth feelings of unity among a community.

(117)   (B) Grounded theory.

Grounded Theory has a different research approach than the rest of social work theories. It applies formal research procedures to social sciences. Typically, a theoretical model comes in the first place; however, grounded theory is primarily based on the collection, categorization, and assessment of data. This data is followed by analysis, after which a theoretical model can be constructed.

(118)   (B) Real-time.

The grounded theory uses a collection of real-time data for analysis. The data is collected by many methods such as interviews, surveys, focus groups, and the study of artifacts and old scripts. Real-time data refers to the information that is delivered right after data collection. Thus, in real-time data and analysis, there is no delay in time. It is an essential aspect of the research approach of the Grounded Theory.

(119)   (C) Microanalysis.

Microanalysis is the method in which researchers code the real-time data collected in different ways such as interviews, surveys, and the study of old scripts in a systematic order. Microanalysis is an essential aspect of the Grounded Theory.

(120)   (A) Grounded Theory.

In the context of social work, Grounded Theory sets up a systematic relationship between universal issues like racial discrimination, geographical remoteness, the socioeconomic gap, and their impacts on individuals. This relationship is quite helpful for social workers to carry out targeted interventions and case identification.

(121)   (B) Inductive reasoning.

Inductive reasoning rather than the use of scientific methods is the unique research approach of Grounded Theory. The theory, in short, is based on the systematic accumulation of data and analysis. Inductive reasoning is based on broad generalizations from specific observations. It is the opposite of deductive reasoning, which is based on logical reasoning.

(122)   (A) Development Theory.

Development theory focuses primarily on the collective effort of individuals for societal development, for which the central idea is social development. Its main principle is to bring all social sectors together on one platform and introduce productive interactions. Therefore, a social worker, under the development theory, works to integrate challenged individuals into society.

(123)   (B) Marginalization.

Marginalization is the term coined for the social exclusion of a group based on the concept of relegation. In marginalization, fundamental human rights, resources, and life opportunities are denied to the excluded group of individuals. Furthermore, social marginalization calls for social unrest and economic instability. When a group is deprived of fundamental rights, they would, at some point, fight for emancipation, as proven through historical events that marginalizing a community or group will lead to socioeconomic imbalance.

(124)   (A) Erikson's Psychosocial Theory

In the context of Erikson's Psychosocial Theory, eight stages of development mark the life of an individual. In each stage, diverse social encounters and crises prompt the individual and how he or she responds to each happening plays a role in shaping their development.

(125)   (B) Will.

According to Erik Erikson's Psychosocial Theory, the second stage of development marks the age of 18 months to 3 years of childhood, i.e., the toddlerhood. It is a vulnerable development stage in which "will" is a key feature as in this stage, children develop a fixed desire to learn new skills.

(126)   (C) Infancy.

By Erik Erikson's Psychosocial Theory, the stage of development marked by infancy is the first 18 months of the child. In this period, the nurturing ability of the child's parents influences the development phase of the child. "Hope" is a key element in this development phase.

(127)   (C) Middle Adulthood.

In middle adulthood, individuals are faced with responsibilities. These years see them focused on career building and fixated on being a contributing part of the social welfare of the society. "Care," and "Responsibility" are the trigger features of this stage of development.

(128)   (B) Young Adulthood.

The stage of development in young adulthood sees the quest for love and companionship with most starting their families. On the contrary, if individuals are unsuccessful in forming satisfying relationships in young adulthood, they fall prey to feelings of loneliness and isolation. In short, the desire for "love" and "companionship" are the key characteristics of this stage of development.

(129)   (B) Pre-schooling.

In the pre-schooling age, i.e., middle childhood, the key feature of the children turns out to be "purpose." They try to evaluate the purpose of their lives from their surroundings and analyze different relationships, especially within the family, in their minds, trying to copy every detail. In this stage of development, their minds are more imaginative than ever, and they may create certain situations in their minds stimulated by real-life incidences.

(130)   (C) Rational Choice Theory.

Rational Choice Theory is based on the concept that the accumulative societal behavior is the product of the conduct of the society's individuals; therefore, society depends upon individual behaviors. George Homans, the founder of Rational Choice Theory, was of the view that there is a profound assembly between economic models and human behaviors.

(131)   (B) George Homans.

George Homans is the known father of the Rational Choice Theory. He delivered the concept that rationality and motivation influence human behaviors to a great extent. These motivations can widely exist in monetary terms as each person evaluates the advantages he/she would gather from the activity and responds analogously. Thus, the benefit of rational choices fuels the social behavior of individuals.

(132)   (C) Rational Choice Theory.

Social behaviors of every person in a society reflect his/her motivation, mostly based on beneficial interests.

(133)   (A) Methodological individualism.

Methodological individualism is a social scientific term. It means that accumulative individual motivations help in explaining the overall social phenomenon, because societal behavior is the product of individual human behaviors.

(134)   (D) Either completeness or transitivity.

Whenever an individual must sort out between two choices, his/her preference is triggered by either completeness or transitivity. Consider that an individual must choose between x and y in a specific scenario. If the individual prefers completeness, he/she would either choose x or y, completely one over another, or ignore both options. On the contrary, consider a choice that must be made between x, y, and z. Then, in case of transitive preference, if the individual prefers x over y, he/she would also alternatively prefer x over z.

(135)   (A) Cognitive Behavioral Therapy.

Cognitive Behavioral Therapy is in a way based on the Rational Choice Theory and is a common choice of social intervention for social workers. The therapy is based on how an individuals' beliefs and societal circumstances influence behaviors and emotions. Social Workers can make use of the Rational Choice Theory to understand the driving motives behind a client's action.

(136)   (C) Rational Choice Theory.

Rational Choice Theory connects economic models and human social behaviors. It cannot be denied that economics plays a significant role in defining individuals' behaviors. Individuals are rationally motivated by money, profit-making, or cost evasion. Usually, individuals calculate profits and losses beforehand, and these motivations influence their decisions.

(137)   (D) Tackle them with a pragmatic approach.

Every social worker needs to address any theoretical situation that may occur with a tangible and practical approach. Using fundamental concepts and simultaneously having the ability to apply pragmatics is vital in the field of social activism.

(138)   (A) Arbitrary.

The choice of models is, practical approaches being applied to and translated from a conceptual understanding. These models rest over the foundation of the analytical substructure. However, the distinctions made to differ from one model to another are hypothetical and subjective, considering there is no particular consensus for it yet.

(139)   (D) A process and an outcome.

Individuals from diverse professions tend to take part in welfare-based projects actively. The most effective response carried out from the social work generally leads to a process and an outcome that follows. Both of these factors are entirely dependent on the difference of approach by these people

(140)  (B) Political justice and community response

From a state's perspective, it is essential to acknowledge that the issue is being dealt with at a macro level. Therefore, the outcome is supposed to have a similar magnitude. The decision to address this issue must entail decisions influenced by the head of state in addition to societal action.

(141)  (C) No, mental health issues and emotional disturbances must be catered for.

Understanding the root of a problem a client may be dealing with makes it essential for the social worker to address the core reason for the problem's existence.  Neglecting the client's subjective accounts complicates the situation even further for the client and the worker.

(142)  (B) Counselling through human influence.

A client's emotions and traumatic experiences must be taken into account to identify the root of the issue. Social therapy and counseling services are intangible and bring a humanely influence over the client. Therefore, improvement objectives are met with expert advice and dictation.

(143)  (A) Cognitive-behavioral therapy.

One of the structures of representation (CRT) emphasizes changing a client's negative perspective on life while also taking their emotions into account. It vitalizes behavioral aspects and cognition and proposes the belief about the interlink that exists between emotions, behaviors, and thoughts.

(144)  (B) To raise self-awareness in clients about their thought process.

The main ulterior motive for CBT is to redefine negative thoughts for a client that may be adversely impacting them. An activity for CBT is Automatic Thought Record, which encourages clients to reflect on their thoughts, raise self-awareness, and change their perspectives for the better.

(145)    (A) Acute mental health crisis.

Crisis intervention model is a delicate model that must be handled with precision and empathic care when dealing with clients who suffer from an acute mental health crisis. Such clients are placed in a mentally vulnerable position due to personal or past events that could result in self-harm or physical harm for others.

(146)    (C) Seven-Stage crisis intervention model.

A social worker that practically applies this model over clients who have post-traumatic stress disorder must understand that the complexity and vitality behind it due to the influence they could have over the client. The well-known technique is the Seven-Stage crisis intervention model. It facilitates social workers to establish goals and aim at progression while making quick decisions.

(147)    (B) Robert and Ottens.

Robert and Ottens had established a set of seven logical guidelines that contained objectives focused on progression for patients suffering from acute mental health crises due to post-traumatic stress disorder. Social workers play essential roles in this model; therefore, they must be quick in decision making and must respond to issues well and precisely.

(148)    (D) Establish psychological contact.

The seven-stage crisis model consists of a total of seven steps that are aimed at the progression and well-being of the client when applied. Thoroughly conducting a danger assessment determines the level of danger the client has to cause self-harm or physically harm others. The first step is the foundation of the stages where the latter rest over. Establishing psychological contact is the second step and depicts the relation and involvement of a social worker and the client when applying therapeutic techniques.

(149)  (A) Therapeutic sessions to ensure the sanity and well-being of the client.

The last stage of the seven-stage crisis intervention model emphasizes the vitality of keeping in check of the client's sanity and well-being through and post the process of treatment. Regular sessions should be able to help clients cope with and counter any issues that may occur later on in their lives. It is the final step towards progression for the client.

(150)  (B) Social workers collaborating with clients to establish and look into narratives that influence and impact the client's lives.

Social workers engage clients in the form of dialogue where the client narrates their experience that is followed by another session of speech. Other possible stories are discussed to assist the social worker in identifying the narratives to which the client is most inclined. Ultimately, the establishment of the above allows the social worker to maintain aims and create a plan for the client's future.

# Test 2: Questions

(1) What kinds of efforts were made in the 19th century in response to the social injustices being carried out?

(A) Mental illness awareness, extirpating child labor, and improving countries containing mass numbers of underprivileged.

(B) Building communities, campaigning against substance abuse, developing education services.

(C) Formation of policies, providing first aid, developing the healthcare sector.

(D) Voluntary healthcare services, building communities, extirpating child labor.

(2) Why was social work still not considered as a separate profession?

(A) It lacked intellectual individuals.

(B) It lacked adequate funding for its development.

(C) It lacked conceptual knowledge to tackle practical issues.

(D) It was made legally unacceptable by the government.

(3) How did social activism revolutionize to being labeled as professional?

(A) Through the application and study of casework and scientific methods.

(B) The government legally registered it as a separate occupation.

(C) Social activism remains as an unrecognized profession.

(D) By incorporating the study of humanity and casework.

(4) When was The National Association of Social Workers (NASW) founded?

(A) 1953.

(B) 1955.

(C) 1995.

(D) 1973.


(5) What were the first medical social workers referred to as?

(A) Medical heroes.

(B) Medical humanitarians.

(C) Hospital almoners.

(D) Philanthropic almoners.


(6) Who founded the US Settlement House Movement?

(A) Mary Stewart.

(B) Jane Addams.

(C) Jane Stewart.

(D) Mary Addams.


(7) Fact Check: A social worker must prioritize the needs of others before their own?

(A) Depending on the country's social policies.

(B) Sometimes.

(C) No.

(D) Yes.

(8) Whitney M Young Jr. was one of the pioneers of professional social activism, of what organization did he become president?

(A) National Association of Social Workers.

(B) Native American Social Workforce.

(C) National Advisory of Social Workers.

(D) North America Social Workers.

(9) From the options listed below by what number of social workers is the expected surge?

(A) 100,000 till 2026.

(B) 1,000,000 till 2026.

(C) 978,000 till 2025.

(D) 1,200,000 till 2026.

(10)    When did the code of ethics for social activism come into being, and when was It revised?

(A) Founded in 1955 and revised in 2018.

(B) Founded in 1973 and revised in 2020.

(C) Founded in 1995 and revised in 2019.

(D) Founded in 1996 and revised in 2017.

(11)    What six core values do the code of ethics comprises of?

(A) Service, human relationships, dignity, competence, social justice, and integrity.

(B) Service, dignity, social justice, empathy, compassion, and human relationships.

(C) Dignity, service, competence, confidence, social justice, and integrity.

(D) Respectfulness, dignity, integrity, human relationships, and social justice.


(12)    What best describes 'social justice'?

(A) Selflessly work every day to assist welfare communities.

(B) Application of in-depth knowledge in resolving political matters by vouching for suppressed members/minorities of society who are in a vulnerable state.

(C) Prioritizing the needs of third-party individuals before their interests.

(D) Understand the fundamentals of collective interest society has by overlooking the differences between individuals.


(13)    From the options listed below, what needs to be built up to signify the importance of human relationships?

(A) Compassion and harmony.

(B) Empathy and unity.

(C) Societal cooperation and harmony.

(D) Societal cooperation and unity.

(14)    Andrew is a social worker whose primary goal lies in assisting others by compromising his needs and prioritizing others in every way. He makes use of his skills by helping individuals selflessly and sometimes without any monetary incentive in return. Which of the code of ethics has Andrew successfully achieved?

(A) Integrity.

(B) Service.

(C) Human relationships.

(D) Dignity.

(15)    Fact check: Social activism is a constricted field that involves no diversity due to lack of professionalism and opportunities.

(A) Yes.

(B) No.

(C) Depends.

(D) Yes. Attempts are being made for the development of social activism.

(16)    Which of the following professions are based on the concept of altruism and selflessness?

(A) Acting.

(B) Teaching.

(C) Social worker.

(D) Nursing.

(17)    Which of the following emotion is affiliated strongly with altruistic help or social work?

(A) Kindness.

(B) Compassion.

(C) Empathy.

(D) Sympathy.


(18)    What is an essential requirement that facilitates a better social work process?

(A) Having a good connection between helper and recipient.

(B) Being sensitive to other's feelings.

(C) Being professional.

(D) Having more altruistic motives.


(19)    In what field is altruism specifically studied to understand why some individuals risk their lives for the benefit of others?

(A) Economics.

(B) Biology.

(C) Psychology.

(D) Sociology.

(20)　Under what circumstances is a social worker required to terminate his or her services immediately?

(A)When the client asks for it.

(B)When the client needs expert or professional help.

(C)When the client's needs are no longer being served.

(D)When the worker is emotionally involved with the client.

(21)　Social workers should follow which guidelines in case of unavailability or discontinuity of their services?

(A) Address their issue first and then discontinue service.

(B)Refer them to a colleague.

(C)Ask the client for an excuse.

(D)Permanently remove themselves from the service.

(22)　What does a social worker need to put time and effort into to resolve?

(A)Client's problems.

(B)Social issues.

(C)Monetary problems.

(D)Personal issues.

(23)    What, according to healthcare workers, is burnout is a condition of?

(A) Heart disease.

(B) Respiratory disease.

(C) Inactivity.

(D) Mental illness.


(24)    What affects social workers due to their encounters with, and being exposed to the stories of victims who have experienced violence?

(A) Burnout.

(B) Discrimination.

(C) Secondary Trauma.

(D) Transference.


(25)    What should social workers should focus on to prevent problems like burnout, compassion fatigue, and secondary trauma?

(A) Financial independence.

(B) Helping more clients.

(C) Working with organizations.

(D) Self-care.

(26)   The psychological concepts of transference and countertransference are common in what type of relationship?

(A) Families and their children.

(B) Older people with their nurses.

(C) Social workers with their clients.

(D) Governments and the public.


(27)   Which one of the following is an example of a professional development activity for social workers?

(A) Exercising.

(B) Learning IT skills.

(C) Yoga.

(D) Camping.


(28)   What are client-client and client-society system competence are essential aspects of?

(A) Dignity.

(B) Worth.

(C) Diversity.

(D) Inclusivity.

(29)   Of the options listed below, what refers to the process of preparing children living in places, out of the home, like foster care.

(A) Self-determination.

(B) Licensing.

(C) Permanency planning.

(D) Client-system competence.


(30)   What do social workers often overlook, forgetting the importance of this role?

(A) Self.

(B) Money.

(C) Power.

(D) Desires.


(31)   Why are self-care activities essential for social workers?

(A) Social work can be tedious.

(B) They have to look after themselves.

(C) They are not dedicated.

(D) They want to enjoy themselves.


(32)   On what basis are people commonly discriminated against?

(A) Sexual orientation.

(B) Gender.

(C) Age.

(D) All of the above.

(33)   What is an integral part of any relationship that helps friends/partners when they are stuck in a difficult situation?

(A) Sympathy.

(B) Empathy.

(C) Financial support.

(D) Mutual support.

(34)   What are a few things we can do to support one another in a relationship?

(A) Appreciate each other's efforts to strengthen the relationship.

(B) Express gratitude, be a good listener, show love, and don't take people for granted.

(C) Set healthy boundaries and limitations.

(D) Support each other emotionally.

(35)   Which of the following mistakes do people often make in a relationship that weakens it?

(A) Stop sharing their secrets with each other.

(B) Sharing intimate details with others.

(C) Try to change or fix the other person.

(D) Demotivate and disregard their goals.

(36)   What is the first thing you should do while promoting new connections?

(A) Focus on the other person and not yourself.

(B) Try to connect become friends immediately.

(C) Say things to make them feel better.

(D) Boost your social life.


(37)   Which of the following factors can deter possible connections?

(A) Being distracted while the other person is talking.

(B) Asking too many questions.

(C) Asking personal questions.

(D) Sharing too much personal information about yourself.


(38)   Which of the following questions should you ask yourself while making new connections?

(A) Should I trust the other person?

(B) Do I feel good after spending time with them?

(C) Is the person respectful towards me?

(D) All of the above.


(39)   What should you avoid doing while someone is talking or sharing with you?

(A) Listen carefully.

(B) Distracted or disinterested.

(C) Interrupt them.

(D) Ask them questions.

(40) Which of the following things do good friends do?

(A) Give you financial help when needed.

(B) They respect, trust, and show interest in your life.

(C) They help you make new friends.

(D) They promote your interests.


(41) Which of the following things can you do to make new connections?

(A) Find common friends.

(B) Increase your social media approach.

(C) Join a club of your interest.

(D) Stalk people.


(42) After making new connections, which of the following things you should do to allow the friendship to evolve?

(A) Give time.

(B) Do similar activities.

(C) Develop similar hobbies.

(D) Become a good listener.

(43)    What is the ability to efficiently handle any situation based on the capacity of your knowledge, skills, and understanding of the task?

(A) Being spontaneous.

(B) Self-evaluation.

(C) Competence.

(D) Eloquence.


(44)    How can social workers increase their level of competence?

(A) Conducting thorough research and acquiring experience.

(B) Following the footsteps of other social workers.

(C) Gaining new clients.

(D) Conducting experiments.


(45)    How does collaboration help in increasing competence?

(A) Building a robust social network.

(B) Transfer of knowledge and new ideas.

(C) Improve process flow.

(D) Developing trust amongst social workers and clients.


(46)    What is a way of enhancing personal and professional skills?

(A) Gaining a client's trust and loyalty.

(B) Self-research and mentorship.

(C) Social networking.

(D) Taking part in social events and gatherings.

(47)　What do social workers come across that differ, with which their level of competence helps them deal?

(A)Clients.

(B)Social events.

(C)Evaluation assessments.

(D)Social issues.


(48)　What is the minimum qualification required to become a social worker?

(A)Bachelor's Degree.

(B)Master's Degree.

(C)Non-Degree Course.

(D)License.


(49)　Which of the following are included in the study of Social Work?

(A)Psychotherapy.

(B)Individual and racial justice.

(C)Ethical guidelines.

(D)All of the above.

(50)   What is the minimum qualification required for the clinical social work profession?

(A) Bachelor's Degree.

(B) Licensure Exam.

(C) Post Graduate Degree.

(D) Training Courses.


(51)   What is meant by applying the acquired knowledge in the practical area of study under close supervision for training?

(A) Professional qualification.

(B) Attending social events.

(C) Field experience.

(D) Enrolling in mentorship programs.


(52)   Who are the licensure examinations administered by?

(A) Association of Social Work Boards.

(B) Association of Professional Social Work.

(C) Social Work Board Association.

(D) Association of Clinical Social Examination.

(53)  Medical/Public health sector, social work research, child welfare, and mental health social worker. What are these examples of?

(A) Code of ethics in social work.

(B) Social work policies.

(C) Different types of social work.

(D) Fields of employment for social workers.

(54)  What is defined as how individuals perceive themselves based on their profession? It represents a person's beliefs, values, attitudes, and behavior.

(A) Professional identity.

(B) Individual identity.

(C) Personal reflection.

(D) Individual opinion.

(55)  Which of the following best describes how a social worker can professionally identify himself?

(A) Identify your personal beliefs and values, use these in the professional field to create your identity.

(B) Acquire the necessary professional knowledge, understand its values and beliefs, and associate them with your personal beliefs to create your professional identity.

(C) Learn about your profession and use your values and beliefs to identity yourself.

(D) Associate yourself with the professional beliefs and values to create a professional identity.

(56)   What helps to create a professional identity for social workers by providing practical experience and exposure.

(A) Formal education.

(B) Obtaining a degree.

(C) Training and mentorship.

(D) Field education.


(57)   Which of the following does not help in developing professional skills?

(A) Supervision.

(B) Self-awareness.

(C) Mentorship.

(D) Personal opinions and judgments.


(58)   Along with professional, ethical, and disciplinary, what other skills must a social worker have?

(A) Moral and values.

(B) Persuasive and fluency.

(C) Intellectual and critical reasoning.

(D) Power to influence.

(59)    Along with professional, what other skills must social workers have to be more competent in their field?

(A) Communication.

(B) Personal growth and development.

(C) Qualitative.

(D) Social networking.

(60)    How can we best describe effective listening?

(A) The ability to listen, empathize, gain trust and confidence, and offer support.

(B) To listen intently and make notes of the account.

(C) To listen carefully, understand, and offer solutions based on your personal opinions

(D) To understand and interpret the problems of your clients and engage in conversation with them.

(61)    Which quality best describes showing empathy, self-awareness, self-reflection, social awareness, and motivation?

(A) Efficient social workability.

(B) Emotional intelligence.

(C) Eloquent social skills.

(D) Active listener.

(62)    Apart from dealing with clients and coming up with new ideas, what personal skills are essential to perform other duties?

(A) Administering, leading.

(B) Task management, fast learner.

(C) Time management, creativity.

(D) Dynamic working, diligence.


(63)    What should social workers should welcome, and not be dismissive of or have reservations against?

(A) Change in the social structure.

(B) Other professionals.

(C) New ideas.

(D) Diversity.


(64)    To have a healthy lifestyle and reduce stress, what is it essential for a social worker to create?

(A) Work-life balance.

(B) Boundaries.

(C) Professional distance.

(D) Scheduled routine.

(65)   At what level is social work conducted on an intermediate scale?

(A) Individual.

(B) Macro.

(C) Micro.

(D) Mezzo.


(66)   Who do workers at mezzo-level interact with?

(A) Communities.

(B) Social groups.

(C) Institutions.

(D) All of the above.


(67)   In which places to social workers involved in mezzo social work usually serve?

(A) Schools.

(B) Hospitals and community centers.

(C) Prisons.

(D) All of the above.


(68)   At Mezzo-level, social workers can work as?

(A) Healthcare workers, doctors, and nurses.

(B) Clinical social workers, community service managers, and group therapists.

(C) Teachers, non-clinical workers, and guards.

(D) None of the above.

(69) Social workers working at the mezzo-level of the field are focused on changing organizations and resolving issues. At what level are their efforts aimed?

(A) Micro.

(B) Macro.

(C) International.

(D) Institutional.


(70) What do social workers working at mezzo-level require substantial experience with?

(A) Interpersonal relationships and community engagement.

(B) Community management and friendliness.

(C) Good listening and communication skills.

(D) All levels of social work and clinical skills.


(71) As a mezzo-level organization, what is the role of the Family Equality Council?

(A) Give equal opportunities to every member of the family.

(B) Deal with family issues such as domestic violence and abuse.

(C) Make policies for minority group families to have equal opportunities.

(D) Provide monetary funds to needy families.

(72)   Which of the following is not an example of formal groups or organizations related to mezzo-level social work?

(A) Self-help Groups.

(B) Correctional facilities.

(C) Educational systems.

(D) Grocery stores.

(73)   Which skills are required by social workers dealing with the dynamics of formal groups at the mezzo-level?

(A) Management, clinical, and planning.

(B) Organizational planning, conflict resolution, and decision-making.

(C) Decision-making, stress handling, and event management.

(D) All of the above.

(74)   The process of change at the mezzo-level takes into account the roles, patterns, interaction styles, and structures of whom?

(A) Individual.

(B) Social workers.

(C) Employees.

(D) Group members.

(75)   Which of the following are the most common types of groups mezzo social workers engage with?

(A) Household, therapy, and self-help groups.

(B) Correctional, non-profits, and interdisciplinary groups.

(C) Educational, healthcare, and self-help groups.

(D) All of the above.


(76)   What needs to be a key component to resolve underlying issues in household groups, allowing it to become most effective?

(A) Individual interaction.

(B) Non-interactive approach.

(C) Interaction between families.

(D) Interaction between neighbors and families.


(77)   Why do the people in a therapy group interact with each other?

(A) Because they know each other.

(B) For therapy purposes.

(C) They need to make friends.

(D) They do not want individual counseling.

(78)   Which of the following is an example of a therapy group social work?

(A) Alcohol recovery.

(B) Grief therapy.

(C) Anger management.

(D) All of the above.


(79)   Why do individuals join peer or self-help groups?

(A) Common friends.

(B) Same problems or interests.

(C) Common goals.

(D) Same working environment.


(80)   What of the following is a trait of peer groups but not therapy groups?

(A) Individuals interact and work together.

(B) Members don't know each other.

(C) Members seek individual assistance.

(D) None of the above.


(81)   Who can help create well-integrated members of society?

(A) Social workers.

(B) Therapists.

(C) Friends.

(D) Families.

(82)   Resulting in positive or negative consequences, what are the roles of families crucial in the development of?

(A) Individuals.

(B) Social norms.

(C) Society.

(D) All of the above.


(83)   What kind of families benefit the community?

(A) Wealthy.

(B) Influential.

(C) Stable.

(D) Healthy.


(84)   Which of the following aspects of families contribute to the welfare of society?

(A) Leaving valuable inheritance.

(B) Help meet basic individual needs.

(C) Make strict family values and rules.

(D) None of the above.

(85)   What best describes what families are the fullest reflection of in the society in which we live, at the very grass-roots level?

(A) Strengths and weaknesses.

(B) Social status and individual roles.

(C) Abilities and disabilities.

(D) All of the above.


(86)   Of the options listed below, who plays a significant role and concentrates all efforts to improve the welfare of families in society?

(A) All members of the families.

(B) Society.

(C) Non-profit organizations.

(D) Social work.


(87)   What is all about exchanging knowledge and sharing ideas by talking to different people and expressing yourself?

(A) Social Networking.

(B) Social Distancing.

(C) Waterboarding.

(D) None of the Above.

(88) What is the process of putting in writing and keeping on file, relevant information about the client, and is an integral part of social work?

(A) Gerrymandering.

(B) Record Keeping.

(C) Osmosis.

(D) Probation.

(89) Besides the prognosis; the intervention plan; the progress of treatment; the social, economic, and health factors that contribute to the situation; and the procedures for termination or referral, what other client records should be kept?

(A) Problem.

(B) Solution.

(C) Social worker's family.

(D) NGO.

(90) Besides development, what else does recording enable the social worker to reflect on their past work and perform course correction accordingly?

(A) Learning.

(B) Deconstruction.

(C) Relief.

(D) None of the Above.

(91)    For social workers who work shifts and work with the same clients as their colleagues, in this light, what is the benefit of adequate record-keeping?

(A) Challenges.

(B) Mistakes.

(C) Argument.

(D) Communication.

(92)    Besides the code of ethics, what other discipline within social work is record keeping associated with?

(A) Rubrics.

(B) Morals.

(C) Values.

(D) Ideas.

(93)    During record keeping, what should social workers ensure is never violated?

(A) Societal.

(B) Ethical.

(C) Discrete.

(D) Variable.

(94)   What are the following statements, all examples of? Honest service to humanity, integrity to your profession, social equality, confidentiality, and client confidence.

(A) Ethical Values.

(B) Manifestos.

(C) Unprofessionalism.

(D) None of the Above.


(95)   Besides maintaining intervention records in file format, which other format is also acceptable?

(A) Conventional.

(B) Electronic.

(C) Any.

(D) None.


(96)   During record-keeping, what type of data is the type that does not meet the needs of clients and doesn't add any value to the service?

(A) Relevant.

(B) Germane.

(C) Irrelevant.

(D) Big.

(97)   What information is taken as the first step of commencing any form of relationship with a client?

(A) Phone Number.

(B) Age.

(C) Consent.

(D) Social Security Number.

(98)   During record keeping, what are the following pieces of information examples of? The client's contact details, consent, progress, any new problems arising during the relationship, and commencement date.

(A) Relevant.

(B) Irrelevant.

(C) Non-essential.

(D) Unimportant.

(99)   When social workers inform clients of their rights, what clause must be laid out clearly before the services are discharged?

(A) Confidentiality.

(B) Ironic.

(C) Morality.

(D) Impartiality.

(100)  By avoidance of jargon and complicated words, what is the social worker developing in their records?

(A) Ambiguity.

(B) Humor.

(C) Clarity of context.

(D) Irony.


(101)  Mixing opinion with one of the options listed below, a social worker would breach the code of conduct?

(A) Facts.

(B) Ideas.

(C) Feelings.

(D) Theories.


(102)  Which type of recording is a way of record keeping that involves the description of real-time/ongoing events – they rely on storytelling?

(A) Verbatim.

(B) Process.

(C) Basic.

(D) Narrative.

(103)  Which type of recording is a way of recording that relies on providing the exact description of the interview?

(A) Verbose.

(B) Minute.

(C) Verbatim.

(D) Narrative.


(104)  Which type of recording is a way of recording that is detail-relevant only and stores session details as paraphrasing?

(A) Process.

(B) Narrative.

(C) Verbatim.

(D) Verbose.


(105)  Which type of recording is a carefully drafted summary of the details, which is suitable for making a distinction between essential facts and the rest of the session?

(A) Process.

(B) Verbatim.

(C) Summary.

(D) Narrative.

(106) Which concept is based on the notion that individuals are to be viewed as components of societies and families rather than being considered as islands, i.e., singular entities?

(A) Conflict Theory.

(B) Systems Theory.

(C) Racialization Theory.

(D) Rational Choice Theory.

(107) Systems theory aids social workers to perceive various social systems and the diverse levels of social environments. Under systems theory, Family systems and individual relations are studied at one level, and institutional and organizational relations are studied at another level. From the options listed below, please name these two levels of social work?

(A) Micro, mezzo.

(B) Mezzo, macro.

(C) Micro, macro.

(D) None of these.

(108) Who constructed the family systems theory with eight interrelated concepts of family systems? The theory states family as a systematic unit wherein each member plays a definite role.

(A) Erik Erikson.

(B) John Bowlby.

(C) Murray Bowen.

(D) Edmund John Bowen.

(109)   On which theory is the concept of social interdependence is based? The concept states that individuals are influenced by a set of correlated systems such as family, institutions, organizations, and even laws and cultures (at a macro level).

(A) Conflict Theory.

(B) Racialization Theory.

(C) Rational Choice Theory.

(D) Systems Theory.


(110)   On which theory is the life model of social work practice as created by Germain and Gitterman based?  It helps examine how individuals adapt to their surroundings. The model helps social workers to investigate the impact of social experiences on the development and decision making of an individual.

(A) Psychodynamic Theory.

(B) Racialization Theory.

(C) Systems Theory.

(D) Psychosocial Theory.


(111)   From the options listed below, what relates to the positive results from the intersection of individuals goals? It directs that if members of a society work in harmony to achieve a common goal, the outcomes are productive.

(A) Interdependence.

(B) Racialization.

(C) Environment.

(D) None of these.

(112)   Which theory interlinks psychology with the spiritual aspects of human beings? The theory emphasizes the goal of reaching a level of consciousness that goes beyond personal character. Primarily, the concept revolves around the objective of promoting unity between spirituality, understanding, and human potential.

(A) Psychological Theory.

(B) Racialization Theory.

(C) Transpersonal Theory.

(D) Conflict Theory.


(113)   Transpersonal theory holds that every individual is capable to self-heal and reach personal growth by diving into inner wisdom and spiritual consciousness. Transpersonal social work revolves around the goal of teaching clients how to harness this ability. What concept of individuals does the theory also focuses on?

(A) The detachment of egos.

(B) Improvement of family systems.

(C) Social isolation.

(D) None of these.


(114)   What are the development stages, based beyond human potential and on spiritual growth associated with? These stages can awaken the highest attributes, such as creativity, wisdom, and altruism in human individuals.

(A) Transpersonal psychology.

(B) Racialization.

(C) Social psychology.

(D) None of these.

(115)   Who is known to be the father of the theory of transpersonal psychology? He was of the view that spiritual experiences should be judged by their impact on individuals rather than being judged on a specific cultural or religious angle.

(A) Erik Erikson.

(B) John Bowlby.

(C) Murray Bowen.

(D) William James.

(116)   From the options listed below, what is/are associated with development psychology? The development psychology revolves around the concept that social experiences are essential for personal growth and survival adaptation.

(A) Socialization Theory.

(B) Bowen's Family Systems Theory.

(C) Erikson's Eight Stages of Development.

(D) Psychosocial Theory.

(117)   What process helps individuals to understand how to function within a group or society? The process of personal development is associated with learning societal norms and standards to function within that group.

(A) Racialization.

(B) Socialization.

(C) Systemization.

(D) None of these.

(118) What arises when individuals cannot develop normal relations within the society? These outcomes are common in individuals that are socially defined, such as the mentally ill, the financially challenged, and the people who have a low socioeconomic position.

(A) Racialization.

(B) Social Deprivation.

(C) Economic Disparity.

(D) None of these.

(119) What kind of problem defines the Tragedy of the Commons? The tragedy occurs by the neglect of the welfare of society by its individuals in the pursuit of personal gain.

(A) Psychological.

(B) Economic.

(C) Social.

(D) None of these.

(120) If a natural resource shared by a group of individuals, and every individual can limitlessly exploit the resource to his/her benefit. From the options listed below, what combination describes this exploitation that is possible in the absence of rules and regulations?

(A) Commons, tragedy.

(B) Assets, disaster.

(C) Capital, misuse.

(D) Assets, tragedy.

(121)   Who penned down "The Tragedy of the Commons." The subject was an American ecologist and advocate of eugenics who strongly warned of the hazards of human overpopulation.

(A) Erik Erikson.

(B) John Bowlby.

(C) Garrett Hardin.

(D) Sigmund Freud.

(122)   Which theory explains that the personality of human beings is a product of conscious and subconscious forces such as desires and beliefs? The theory has a close association with Sigmund Freud's Psychoanalytic Therapy that aids in revealing unconscious thoughts and desires of individuals.

(A) Psychosocial Theory.

(B) Socialization Theory.

(C) Psychodynamic Theory.

(D) Systems Theory.

(123)   Who constructed the psychoanalysis therapy to treat mental illnesses? The therapy was also useful to explain human behaviors in social environments. The subject was of the view that childhood experiences influenced individuals' personalities.

(A) Sigmund Freud.

(B) John Bowlby.

(C) Murray Bowen.

(D) Erik Erikson.

(124)   Which theory states that individuals' conscious mental activity tries to hide their true incentives? That is to say that minds are naturally deceptive. However, the individuals themselves are also unable to understand when they are deceiving themselves.

(A) Bowen's Family Systems Theory.

(B) Erikson's Eight Stages of Development.

(C) Psychodynamic Theory.

(D) Socialization Theory.


(125)   Who constructed the impactful mind model? According to the mind model, the human mind can be divided into three layers. These layers include the conscious, the subconscious or preconscious, and the unconscious.

(A) Erik Erikson.

(B) Murray Bowen.

(C) Sigmund Freud.

(D) John Bowlby.


(126)   According to the mind model, Sigmund Freud suggests that the human mind can be divided into three layers; the conscious, the preconscious or the subconscious, and the unconscious. In which layer do the memories of an individual exist?

(A) The conscious.

(B) The preconscious or the subconscious.

(C) The unconscious.

(D) Both (A) and (B).

(127) Sigmund Freud developed a more structural model of the mind. This model coexists with the ideas of unconsciousness and consciousness. According to this model, the human mind can be divided into three segments. What are these segments?

(A) The unconscious, the subconscious, and the conscious.

(B) The id, the ego, and the superego.

(C) Desires, beliefs, and memories.

(D) None of these.


(128) What is the segment of Sigmund Freud's structural mind model that functions at the level of unconsciousness? This segment primarily focuses on the desires and motivations of an individual.

(A) The id.

(B) The Ego.

(C) The Superego.

(D) Both (B) and (C).


(129) According to Sigmund Freud's mind model, the id segment of the human mind includes two key motivations. From the options listed below, please name both?

(A) Ego and superego.

(B) Love and companionship.

(C) Survival and death instincts.

(D) None of these.

(130) What acts as an intermediary between the real world and the unrealistic id segment of the human mind? It functions as a check for the id. It is developed in early childhood years, and is the decision-making constituent of human personality according to Sigmund Freud's model.

(A) The ego.

(B) The superego.

(C) Both (A) and (B).

(D) None of these.


(131) In which segment of the Sigmund Freud's structural mind model are life principles and sense of morality are linked? The segment is related to the unconsciousness and is evolved overtime through standard learning from the environment and society.

(A) Ego.

(B) Superego.

(C) Id.

(D) None of these.


(132) Central to his constructed therapy, psychoanalysis idea, what does Sigmund Freud suggest that the personality of an adult individual is the product of which of his/her experiences?

(A) Young adulthood.

(B) Childhood.

(C) Middle adulthood.

(D) None of these.

(133)  In social work, which practice is helpful to treat mental ailments such as drug addiction, schizophrenia, and sexual deviance?  It is an efficient method that helps individuals to grow up into better versions of themselves. According to this approach, it is considered that childhood traumas and general experiences have a profound impact on individuals' lives.

(A) Psychoanalytic.

(B) Rational.

(C) Psychosocial.

(D) Cognitive.


(134)  Segments of the unconscious mind, the id, and the superego are in constant struggle with the conscious segment of the mind, the ego. The human mind caters to this situation by using the ego's use of defense mechanisms that are the psychological strategies. What does this conflict create?

(A) Confidence.

(B) Anxiety.

(C) Tranquility.

(D) None of these.


(135)  What is the transpersonal self-posited to be the nucleus of?

(A) Consciousness.

(B) Unconsciousness.

(C) Superego.

(D) Ego.

(136)   Which of the models is considered the oldest 'evidence-based practices' in social activism?

(A)Cognitive-Behavior Therapy.

(B)Task-Centered Practice.

(C)Narrative Practice Therapy.

(D)Crisis Intervention Model.


(137)   Choose what best defines Task-Centered Practice?

(A)Client-worker collaboratively establishing attainable objectives to counter the problem.

(B)Social workers engage clients in tasks to distract them from the problem itself.

(C)An attempt made by the social worker to find potential solutions to the client's problem without identifying its root.

(D)Sessions are given by the social worker to counsel the client and propose a solution through an exchange of dialogue.


(138)   What do task-centered practices give importance to?.

(A)Client's preferences.

(B) Client's problems.

(C)Client's emotional trauma.

(D)Client's personal relations.

(139)  What is the last phase for the Task-Centered Practice model?

(A) Defining the problem and plotting possible solutions collectively.

(B) Creating an agreement between the worker and the client.

(C) Assessing whether or not goals are being accomplished.

(D) Frequent follow-up sessions to reinforce objectives and ensure the client's wellbeing.


(140)  What best defines the importance of the globalization of social work?

(A) Diversity in every aspect of social activism.

(B) Collectively being able to respond to challenges that could have impacts worldwide.

(C) Assists countries with developing economies.

(D) Rise in the human development index in most countries.


(141)  In relevance to what is globalization, the international unification of all processes?

(A) Global awareness, empathy, and practicality.

(B) Global enlightenment, fundamental understanding, and practical approach.

(C) Healthcare facilitation, management, and awareness.

(D) Economic production, distribution, and consumption.

(142)  Of the options listed below, which can identify proof of social work being recognized as an international profession?

(A) Social work has still not been identified as an international profession.

(B) Global awareness leading to the establishment of recognition.

(C) Countries with established economies have labeled social work as an international profession.

(D) Common international culture and collective global awareness.


(143)  What are the three general levels of response to global issues?

(A) Local, national, and international.

(B) Micro-level, mezzo level, and macro-level.

(C) Problem identification, conceptual understanding, and practical application.

(D) Problem identification, psychological contact, and attainment of objectives.


(144)  For a developmental problem to arise and exist on a regional scale, which of the following renowned organizations or authorities would respond to address the problem?

(A) National Governments.

(B) United Nations.

(C) European Union.

(D) World Welfare Organization.

(145)  How do the IFRC and its national societies provide assistance and support to communities?

(A)Through the coalition, assistance, and reference of other world organizations.

(B)Preaching to communities about necessary guidelines and precautions.

(C)Provision of experienced volunteers that practice welfare-improvement methods while they interact within the community.

(D)Awareness campaigns related to health to attain attention from other world organizations.


(146)  Identify the correct statement.

(A)Despite significant health developments, the death rate for malaria and measles continues to rise.

(B)While there have been several improvements in global healthcare, reaching primary objectives at the community-level remains a challenge.

(C)Global health has mounted its peak of development where little to no health challenges appear to be a hindrance.

(D)The IFRC and its societies are not limited to providing health-related services solely.


(147)  What are the three primary aims for IFRC?

(A)Facilitate communities in need; collaborate with world leaders, and improving healthcare services.

(B)Identifying the problem, expanding primary health care services, and creating social awareness campaigns.

(C)Identifying illnesses, facilitating communities in need, and creating awareness programs.

(D)Expansion of primary healthcare services, improvement of healthcare, and constructive action on several aspects linked to good health.

(148) At which levels does the IFRC collaborate with other organizations to improve health, economic and social conditions?

(A) Primary and secondary level.

(B) Mezzo and Macro Level.

(C) Regional and international level.

(D) Regional and Macro Level.


(149) Which of the following is not an IFRC partnership initiative?

(A) Global tuberculosis eradication initiative.

(B) Chair of the alliance for malaria prevention.

(C) The global polio eradication initiative.

(D) Global measles initiative.


(150) What does IFSW stand for?

(A) International Federation of Social Workers.

(B) Interesting facts for Social Workers.

(C) International forces of Social Workers.

(D) Interlinked Federation of Social Workers.

# Test 2: Answers & Explanations

(1) (A) Mental illness awareness, extirpating child labor, and improving countries containing mass numbers of underprivileged.

Post the events of the American Civil War, significant reforms came about recognizing more forms of injustice that occurred as a consequence of the war. Changes such as creating awareness about mental health, child labor being eradicated, and countries that were struck with poverty were aimed towards development.

(2) (C) It lacked conceptual knowledge to tackle practical issues.

Though more social awareness was created by the 19th century and many social activists opted to volunteer for betterment toward society, philanthropy or social work was still not deemed as an occupation. In-depth knowledge and comprehension of every distinct aspect were required to tackle and work with practical scenarios, which it then lacked.

(3) (A) Through the application and study of casework and scientific methods.

University programs were launched where individuals were committed to applying practical knowledge over theoretical situations. The study of casework continued while more scientific methods were incorporated into the study of philanthropy, which ultimately led to the professionalization of social work.

(4) (B) 1955.

The establishment of The National Association of Social Workers (NASW) took place in 1955, which played an essential role in the promotion of social activism and bringing it closer to being labeled as a 'profession.' Its study consisted of progressive social policies, a chance at academically learning about social work through formal education, and professional development.

(5) (C) Hospital almoners.

During the initial stages of the professionalization of social activism, the first medical social activists were referred to as hospital almoners, primarily because they worked in the field of medicine and practiced in relevant premises.

(6) (B) Jane Addams.

Jane Addams was a young student who aimed to diminish poverty in the region by creating settlement houses in poverty-stricken cities for social workers. She was able to achieve her visionary goals by founding the US Settlement House Movement. Thirty-two different states contained 413 settlements created by the movement in an attempt to create a better lifestyle for the less fortunate.

(7) (D) Yes.

As a social worker, it is obligatory to comply with the code of ethics and have the basic core values deeply instilled. Placing and catering to a client's needs before your own is an act of selflessness, which is an essential element that is needed to be a social worker, regardless of the discipline in which you wish to work.

(8) (A) National Association of Social Workers.

The list for notable influencers who played a vital role in the establishment of civil rights movements and social welfare organizations is quite extensive. One of the first instigators, Whitney M. Young Jr, went on to be the president of the National Association of Social Welfare.

(9) (A) 100,000 till 2026.

With the increase of social workers working in respective domains to tackle and cater to different aspects of social welfare, there has been a rise in demand for such workers despite several organizations that currently operate and exist. US Bureau of Labor Statistics predicts the number of social workers to rise by more than 100,000 until 2026. The recent pandemic crisis is a notable example of a rising demand for social activists to assist in combating this global issue.

(10)    (D) Founded in 1996 and revised in 2017

The nature of the setting a social worker may work in could vary diversely from one branch to another. Regardless of their kind of interest in welfare assistance, every worker must comply with the code of ethics formed by the National Association of Social Workers (NASW), which was established in 1996 and revised in 2017.

(11)    (A) Service, human relationships, dignity, competence, social justice, and integrity

The National Association of Social workers had released an outline on the code of ethics that every social worker must possess or develop in themselves in terms of qualities. It is a code of conduct that vitalizes over six fundamental core values that consist of service, human relationships, dignity, competence, social justice, and integrity, all of which must be the motive of every worker to achieve and apply while they work.

(12)    (B) Application of in-depth knowledge in resolving political matters by vouching for suppressed members/minorities of society who are in a vulnerable state.

Social Justice is a prominent feature in the code of ethics that every worker must possess. Poverty, discrimination, inequalities, and unjust wage scale differences are all catered by social workers who wish to serve justice. The ability to advocate on behalf of the suppressed members of society and enlighten people about the fundamental rights they have is what social justice preaches.

(13)    (C) Societal cooperation and harmony.

The act of engaging individuals who can work in an integrated manner towards the betterment of society, encouraging, and assisting one another is what defines the importance of human relationships. Consistent cooperation by society and bringing harmony in the region is the main objective when mastering the art of this core value.

(14)    (B) Service.

The hypothetical scenario given stated how 'Andrew' was implying service as a code of conduct in his professional life as a social worker. He is consistently determined to aid others in improving the quality of their lives and address social issues such as child abuse, substance abuse, and residential instability.


(15)    (B) No.

The consistent dedication by the trailblazers of social activism is the reason why humanitarian services are considered professional. Social activism is a diverse field, contains endless opportunities, and is one of the fast-growing occupations.


(16)    (C) Social worker.

Social work's core concept is to professionally help those who are in need to the best of one's abilities. People who are social workers have strong humanitarian values.


(17)    (C) Empathy.

Even though social work requires many social values, empathy is one such emotion that is strongly affiliated with altruistic help because it helps in considering the other person's perspective and situation, further creating compassionate caring.


(18)    (A) Having a good connection between helper and recipient

Being aware of the needs of others is one of the primary motivations for social workers, and this helps to identify with the person needing help. Thus, social workers need to develop a connection with their client so that latter can be better facilitated.

(19)    (D) Sociology.

Altruism is studied in various fields, but in sociology, it is particularly studied to understand the behavior of individuals in particular societies in which they endanger their lives for the well-being of others.


(20)    (C) When the client's needs are no longer being served.

Under the guidelines provided by The Code of Ethics of the National Association of Social Workers, when the client's needs are not being met, the social worker should not waste time and resources by prolonging the professional relationship.


(21)    (B) Refer them to a colleague.

If a social worker has some disruption due to the unavailability of electronic communication or personal issues, then the worker must refer the client to a colleague for the continuity of services. They can also inform the organization.


(22)    (B) Social issues.

Social work requires a great deal of motivation and passion because a social worker must put other's needs before his own. A social worker volunteers time to resolve social issues so that vulnerable people are assisted.


(23)    (C) Inactivity.

Healthcare experts define social work burnout as a condition of inactivity. It is a very natural outcome of social work due to the labor and resource-intensive nature of the profession. Many practitioners from around the world leave the profession due to this burnout. The nature of social work is very labor-intensive and can take a toll on the physical health of social workers. They become lethargic and incapable of performing their duties adequately due to burning out.

(24)    (C) Secondary Trauma

Secondary trauma occurs when individuals like social workers work with people who have experienced some trauma firsthand, exposing them to disturbing details of those traumatic events. Psychologically, this indirect exposure to trauma through a narrative or an account can lead to secondary trauma for the social worker. Professionals debate secondary trauma as being a reaction rather than an actual disorder. Nevertheless, it affects millions of social workers all over the world.

(25)    (D) Self-care.

Self-care refers to activities and practices that social workers can engage in to look after themselves. Practicing self-care enables social workers to identify potential challenges and manage them healthily. It also allows exposure to their vulnerabilities, such as tendencies for compassion fatigue, secondary trauma, or burnout.

(26)    (C) Social workers with their clients.

Social workers are engaged in supervisory relationships with their clients and the community. The concepts of transference and countertransference help social workers understand the unconscious nature of interactions, particularly with clients that are from severely regressed and violent backgrounds. Clients are likely to open up about traumatic experiences with the social worker. They direct their emotions and feelings towards them unconsciously, which can mentally affect the social worker.

(27)    (B) Learning IT skills.

The process of professional development for social workers is not only limited to formal learning activities like training and workshops. Any activity which helps them develop new skills to facilitate their services can be considered a professional development activity like learning IT skills and SEO optimization, which can help them promote their services to clients through the internet. The other skills that are listed do not directly contribute to professional development as they are more focused on personal and health development.

(28)    (D) Inclusivity.

An essential aspect of inclusivity is dealing with client-client and client-society system competencies. Social workers need to indoctrinate their clients with the responsible agency (self-determination) as their understanding helps social workers be better at their job and be more inclusive.

(29)    (C) Permanency Planning.

Permanency planning is the process of assessing and preparing children living in out-of-home placements like foster care – this helps foster healthy social connections and helps the child into adulthood. It requires a care plan that centers on the best interests of the child with a consistent assessment of the child's requirements and how he will be able to achieve his best self.

(30)    (A) Self.

Social workers must appreciate the importance of the role of the self in social work. It demands that the social workers utilize their knowledge-base, skillset, and values in social interventions. Quite often, social workers overlook the importance of individual roles and lose themselves to institutional agendas and visions. They do not recognize that it is vital to keep their physical and mental health in a good state so that it does not affect their ability to perform their job effectively.

(31)    (B) They have to look after themselves.

The physical and mental wellbeing of social workers is an essential prerequisite for efficient social work. Social workers cannot be expected to provide compassionate care and guidance to society without being compassionate to themselves. Therefore, social workers need to understand basic self-care principles and techniques to look after themselves better.

(32)    (D) All of the above.

Various forms of discrimination exist in society today. People are discriminated against based on their age, gender, culture, ethnicity, language, sexual orientation, and class. Thus, all of the options for this question are accurate.

(33)    (D) Mutual support.

Emotional support strengthens a relationship because it allows you to be there for your friend or partner in times of need. Mutual support helps people face difficult or stressful situations, which strengthens their relationship.

(34)    (B) Express gratitude, be a good listener, show love, and don't take people for granted.

Supporting each other is an integral part of any relationship. Partners/friends can support each other by listening, appreciating their efforts, thanking each other for the things they have done, and most of all, appreciating their presence in their lives.

(35)    (C) Try to change or fix the other person.

People in a relationship often tend to mold the other person into the shape of their expectations and wishes. It is essential to understand that we cannot force anyone to change, and we need to accept who they are. We can help them overcome their shortcomings if they realize it, and instead of trying to 'fix' them and support them in every way possible.

(36)    (A) Focus on the other person and not yourself.

Promoting new connections is a challenge for those who are not social. However, if you are making efforts to form new connections, the first thing you need to do is to shift the focus to the other person by asking them questions about their lives to try to get to know them better.

(37)    (D) Sharing too much personal information about yourself.

Even though promoting new connections is all about getting to know one another, things must be taken steadily. You cannot overwhelm the other person by sharing private information about yourself, as sharing information must depend on the level of friendliness that is developing.

(38)    (D) All of the above.

While making new connections, you can ask yourself all of these questions before moving forward with the relationship, so that you feel comfortable with the other person.  The other person must allow you to be your authentic self, make you feel good and genuine, and be supportive and respectful towards your needs.


(39)    (B) Distracted or disinterested.

It is incredibly upsetting to be distracted or show disinterest when someone is talking to you. When making new connections, it is essential to show the other person that you care and are listening.  During this time, you should avoid using a cell phone or other means of distraction.


(40)    (B) They respect, trust, and show interest in your life.

Good friends do many things for you, but friendship is built on respect, trust, and authenticity. Without these, friendships cannot flourish. Good friends will make you feel comfortable, trusted, and respected before anything else.


(41)    (C) Join a club of your interest.

One of the best ways to make new connections is to find people with common interests. Joining a club of your interest lets you meet people with the same interests or hobbies, allowing you to cover more ground and become more comfortable talking about your shared interests.  You can also attend concerts, lectures, and events to meet new people.


(42)    (A) Give time.

Every new relationship requires time to nurture. Becoming a good listener requires time and patience; therefore, with new connections,  give them time to evolve organically rather than forcing the growth.

(43)    (C) Competence.

A social worker must possess the ability to handle complex situations that may arise during service. It is not just about living by the book but rather about how effectively you can perform tasks and deal with challenges.

(44)    (A) conducting thorough research and acquiring experience.

Every social worker must do extensive research work and go through the levels of formal education to increase their level of competency. As a social worker, you should never stop learning as new things can be used to your benefit, and the best way to be more adept is by experience, learning from your mistakes, and making this part of your personal development and growth.

(45)    (B) Transfer of knowledge and new ideas.

Social workers engage with their clients as well as other members from different communities and groups. This collaboration allows them to learn new ways of performing their social duties while the exchange of ideas enables them to increase their competency level and enhance their skills.

(46)    (B) Self-research and mentorship.

Social workers need to improve their professional and personal development continually. There are many ways to enhance these skills, such as self-research and mentorships, which can hone the development of individuals from different walks of life. Other options include seeking help from professional and more experienced social workers, joining a mentorship program, or taking an online course.

(47)    (D) Social issues.

There are many social issues that social workers encounter. While it is not easy to confront or tackle such situations, you must be competent enough to handle these challenges. Competency helps you deal with social issues in a better way allowing your clients to have a better experience.

(48)    (A) Bachelor's Degree.

The minimum requirement for most of the countries is a bachelor's degree in Social Work. Although there are variations regarding the minimum requirement, depending on the state in which you live, most offer entry-level social work jobs to individuals with a bachelor's degree in Social Work.

(49)    (D) All of the above.

A degree in Social Work covers all of these topics and more; therefore, social workers should be familiar with these courses required to practice social services.

(50)    (B) Licensure Exam.

If you want to pursue a professional career in clinical social work, you are required to obtain a post-graduate degree as well as passing a social work licensure examination. The qualification requirements may vary for some states, and however, once you receive the license, you will be eligible to practice clinical social work as a professional.

(51)    (C) Field experience.

Getting field experience is a prerequisite to becoming a qualified graduate. Field experiences can help social workers receive the required training, exposure, and experience to proceed further and start their careers. Field experience teaches you the necessary skills required at a professional level of social work.

(52)    (A) Association of Social Work Boards.

The Association of Social Work Boards conducts standardized exams for different categories of qualifications such as Bachelor's, Master's, Generalist, and Clinical. Social workers are required to register themselves and take the exam on the scheduled date.

(53)    (D) Fields of employment for social workers.

Social workers have several options available for employment. They can join a welfare organization or support group; they can work in a community center or as an individual licensed practitioner.

(54)    (A) Professional identity.

The ability to correctly identify yourself in terms of your profession is called professional identity. It is based on several factors which include a reflection on an individual's personal beliefs and values, the profession's beliefs, and values, and how well you can manage to align your values with those of your profession.

(55)    (B) Acquire the necessary professional knowledge, understand its values and beliefs, and associate them with your personal beliefs to create your professional identity.

It is vital to ensure that your personal beliefs do not hamper the decisions or your actions in a professional environment. You should align your personal as well as professional beliefs to create a unique professional identity.

(56)    (D) Field education.

Field education allows social workers to gain the necessary experience under close supervision. It helps them to improve as individuals and shapes their learning, preparing them for the professional world.

(57)    (D) Personal opinions and judgments.

As a social worker, you must refrain from mixing your personal views and negative judgments regarding the work. Your professional practice should be independent of any sort of reservations or judgments that you might have against the profession or your clients.

(58)   (C) Intellectual and critical reasoning.

One of the essential professional skills that all social workers should have is the ability to think on an intellectual level and effectively use critical reasoning to have logical discussions with their clients or other social workers.

(59)   (B) Personal growth and development.

It is not just about being professional and learning all the skills required to do your job as a social worker. It is about becoming a better person and allowing yourself to be open to positive changes, which will lead to your personal growth—understanding the importance of developing yourself along the way as this will help you to become more efficient.

(60)   (A) The ability to listen, empathize, gain trust and confidence, and offer support.

Effective listening is an essential skill for all social workers. You must understand what your clients say as if not, you will not be able to provide them the best solutions. The ability to feel how they are feeling and to empathize, will not only make them feel better but will help you relate more to what they are going through.

(61)   (B) Emotional intelligence.

Emotional intelligence is a crucial skill that every person should have. This skill is often overlooked or misunderstood. Emotional intelligence helps to build better relationships and encourages a healthy work environment. Social workers with high emotional intelligence tend to work better with their clients, finding it to gain their trust and develop an understanding.

(62)   (C) Time management, creativity.

Since social workers have other duties as well, it is necessary to manage time according to daily tasks. If you manage your time effectively, you can finish all your tasks as per your schedule. On the other hand, it is important to be innovative and creative, to come up with different solutions, and enhance your knowledge.

(63)    (D) Diversity.

There are people present from different ethical, cultural, racial, and religious backgrounds. Social workers must not hold any personal grudges against anyone despite their background. They must show respect to people from all walks of life and treat everyone equally and fairly. It is also crucial not to insult anybody's customs and traditions.

(64)    (A) Work-life balance.

Stress is a part of any job, including social work. Social workers feel stressed out and exhausted, which negatively impacts physical as well as mental health. It is advisable to create and maintain a healthy work-life balance, as this will help you handle the pressure of the job and give you enough personal space for your leisure or family time.

(65)    (D) Mezzo.

The field of social work is divided into three main categories, namely, micro, mezzo, and macro. Mezzo is the level of social work where activities are conducted on an intermediate scale, which lies between micro and macro.

(66)    (D) All of the above.

Mezzo-level social services include serving communities, institutions, small groups, and neighborhoods to resolve their issues for the welfare of society.

(67)    (D) All of the above.

People working at mezzo-level interact with groups of people that can vary from a small and intimate group to larger groups such as in hospitals, prisons, and community centers.

(68)   (B) Clinical social workers, community service managers, and group therapists.

These professions are a few examples related to mezzo-level social work where people can help others deal with their issues on a larger scale and in groups, teaching us that we can deal with our problems together.

(69)   (D) Institutional.

Mezzo-level social workers are more focused on changing organizations and groups as they are passionate about resolving issues at an institutional level rather than working one-to-one. Social workers play different roles to achieve this goal.

(70)   (A) Interpersonal relationships and community engagement.

Individuals working at mezzo-level social work are required to interact with a variety of clients from small groups to medium-sized businesses, local communities, schools, and organizations, requiring skills that can bring about institutional change rather than individual.

(71)   (C) Makes policies for minority group families to have equal opportunities.

Many mezzo-level organizations help make society better for everyone. The Family Equality Council is one such non-profit organization that targets minority group families to cater to their social issues such as housing, employment, foster care, education, and equity.

(72)   (D) Grocery stores.

Social workers related to mezzo-level formal groups and organizations mostly include non-profit institutes that take care of the most vulnerable people of our society. They are dedicated to making their lives better.

(73)  (B) Organizational planning, conflict resolution, and decision-making.

As a social worker working at mezzo-level will often work with formal groups and organizations. To understand the dynamics of how these groups work and should work, social workers must have the skills mentioned above to facilitate change amongst them.


(74)  (D) Group members.

Social workers at the mezzo-level are focused on midlevel intervention. The needs of the groups or organizations are met by drawing resources from individual members, which is why the process of change considers the roles and interaction styles of group members.


(75)  (A) Household, therapy, and self-help groups.

Social workers at the mezzo-level work with various groups and provide quality service to the best of their abilities. They must understand the dynamics of each group and come up with a relevant solution. Among the many groups they work with, those mentioned are the most common.


(76)  (C) Interaction between families.

Families of household groups include members living in the same household. Social workers interact with these families to identify the underlying issue. Sometimes multiple families are involved in making a more extensive group by social workers, while each family is considered an individual entity.


(77)  (B) For therapy purposes.

Therapy groups consist of people who do not belong to the same family; they are practically strangers. People in a therapy group are there to receive therapy, and there is no other objective of the group.

(78)    (D) All of the above.

The groups mentioned above are examples of the common types of group therapy. Individuals in group therapies are usually going through the same issues, such as an alcohol recovery group consists of anonymous people recovering from substance abuse or are alcoholics. People in therapy groups have no relationship with one another.

(79)    (B) Same problems or interests.

Peer or self-help groups consist of people interacting or working together who have common problems or interests. These groups hope that communicating with one another to open new opportunities for all the members.

(80)    (A) Individuals interact and work together.

The main difference between therapy and peer groups is that in therapy groups, people only interact with each other for the sake of therapy and individual assistance. However, in peer or self-help groups, individuals tend to use group and teamwork for handling matters.

(81)    (D) Families.

Families are the building block of society as they help instill societal values and norms and determine an individual's role in the overall society. They provide support and care for vulnerable individuals.

(82)    (C) Society.

Even though individuals are affected by families, the crucial development of society depends on families as a unit. Families play an essential role in influencing negative and positive consequences in society.

(83)  (D) Healthy.

Members of healthy families are the ones who are genuinely able to contribute to the welfare of society. Good family values help motivate people to improve the lives of vulnerable people, as they feel responsible for others in the community.

(84)  (B) Help meet basic individual needs.

Families contribute to society by facilitating a system that allows them to meet the needs of those who cannot tend to themselves. They do not discriminate between the sick, the healthy, the minors, or the elderly as they look out for every member of society.

(85)  (A) Strengths and weaknesses.

How families function determines the kind of impact the members will have as a whole. For this reason, families reflect the weaknesses and strengths present in our society and allow us to study and improve them.

(86)  (D) Social work.

Social work ensures the survival of the society as a whole, working on every level from micro to mezzo, where social workers are involved with individuals, families, and groups to provide their services. The field of social helps improve the lives of those related to these groups.

(87)  (A) Social Networking.

Networking is all about exchanging knowledge, sharing ideas, and talking to different people – it involves expression. You can tell people about your interests and vice versa, but the sharing of information will help you learn new things.

(88)    (B) Record Keeping.

The Social Work Dictionary (2014) defines recording as, "the process of putting in writing and keeping on file relevant information about the client; the problem; the prognosis; the intervention plan; the progress of treatment; the social, economic, and health factors that contribute to the situation; and the procedures for termination or referral." The recording is an integral part of social work practice. Social activism makes it vital to have a client database which includes their statistics and any other details to be recorded, ensuring meticulous precision in handling of the problem which allows the worker to keep track on all of the client's information and respond to their problems effectively

(89)    (A) Problem.

According to the Social Work Dictionary of 2014, record-keeping involves keeping relevant information on the client, the problem, the prognosis, the intervention plan, the progress of treatment, the social, economic, and health factors.

(90)    (A) Learning.

Recording helps in learning and development as you can reflect upon your previous work and correct any mistakes in the future, in addition to finding new solutions or methods of dealing with situations.

(91)    (D) Communication.

The method of record-keeping helps in effective communication among social workers. Most social workers have to work in shifts and might need to keep a record of their work for the next worker to update them regarding the events of the day.

(92)    (C) Values.

Values and codes of ethics are governing principles and cornerstones of the social work discipline, and combined with record-keeping, they maintain transparency.

(93)   (B) Ethical.

Ethical values form a foundation in the social work discipline, and cannot be violated in any way by the social worker.


(94)   (A) Ethical Values.

Some ethical values include an honest service to humanity, integrity to your profession, social equality, confidentiality, and client confidence. They are indispensable traits for a social worker.


(95)   (B) Electronic.

In the digital age, social workers have the freedom to either store their records digitally or stick to conventional file-keeping practices. Many modern social worker organizations resort to a blend of both for maximum efficiency.


(96)   (C) Irrelevant.

While recording, it is imperative that the recordings not include irrelevant data that does not meet the needs of the clients or add any value to the service. It helps social workers discharge their duties most efficiently and saves time on having to sort out point-based facts about the client to produce an effective solution.


(97)   (C) Consent.

Even though record-keeping may be essential in most cases, what is vital to a social worker is to ensure they have their client's full consent. Consent is a crucial aspect of record keeping. The client needs to be well informed and aware of the collection of their information and how it will be used. It ensures that they are comfortable with the process.

(98)    (A) Relevant.

The recording should contain complete information relevant to the case, such as the client's contact details, consent, progress, any new problems arising during the relationship, and the commencement date.

(99)    (A) Confidentiality.

The bridge of trust between the client and the worker must be maintained and protected at all costs. If the client, at any point, loses their trust in the worker, it may complicate things for both parties. The confidentiality clause in social activism offers assurance to the client that all the information that they choose to give away to the social worker will be in "safe hands." They can freely express themselves without fear and hesitation.

(100)   (C) Clarity of Context.

If you are maintaining a record of your writings, it is crucial to ensure that the written content is clear and easy to understand. Avoid using jargon and complicated words that people may not be able to comprehend as this promises a clarity of context to those who follow in the case.

(101)    (A) Facts.

It will be against the code of conduct if you form a judgment based on the opinion of another person. For example, people may have different views on various subject matters, such as whether a person suffering from mental health problems should be allowed to be alone or not.

(102)    (D) Narrative.

Narrative recordings describe real-time or ongoing events. They represent a scenario according to the way we speak, as if in the form of storytelling. Narrative recording involves providing a continuous description of the events that take place during observation as they occur in real-time. It is not limited to a particular incident, but rather encompasses all events taking place in a given time frame.

(103)   (C) Verbatim.

This record-keeping method provides the exact description of the interview. It is an account of everything that each party involved had spoken during the session without any changes or fabrications.

(104)   (A) Process.

Process recording contains details of the session but with paraphrasing. This type of record only keeps the relevant information and preserves this according to the sequence in which the series of events or sessions took place.

(105)   (C) Summary.

A summary recording is suitable for distinguishing important facts from the entire session. It is a carefully drafted summary of the narrative as a whole. The advantage of summary recording is that it reduces excess data and irrelevant information by filtering out the facts.

(106)   (B) Systems Theory.

Systems Theory focuses on the impact of social life on an individual. According to this theory, social systems such as family, institutions, organizations, and laws govern the influences on the life of an individual.

(107)   (A) Micro, mezzo.

Under Systems Theory, family systems are systematic units at the micro-level. On the other hand, institutions and organizations are systematic elements at the mezzo level. These systematic units interrelate with one another to engender an impact on the lives of individuals.

(108)   (C) Murray Bowen.

Murray Bowen created the family systems theory that aims at restoring healthy relationships within family systems. Bowen was of the view that the family stands as an emotional systematic unit that binds the family members together in various aspects.

(109)   (D) Systems Theory.

The concept of interdependency is closely related to the Systems Theory. This concept defines the mutual dependence of individuals over one another and on the environment. Both are central to the idea that autonomous elements, i.e., individuals make up a community that, in turn, has a direct impact on individuals' lives.

(110)   (C) Systems Theory.

The assembly of the life model on the systems theory aids social workers to examine how individuals fit in with their surroundings. The theoretical model is also central to the observation of how individuals adapt to the restrictions and toxicity present in their environment.

(111)   (A) Interdependence.

Positive interdependence is central to collective growth and development of individuals. These individuals tend to share common goals, and the success is dependent on individual participation; however, framed in the collaborative efforts. On the contrary, negative interdependence is central to the idea that individuals can only obtain their specific goals by competing against other members of society.

(112)   (C) Transpersonal Theory.

The transpersonal theory explains the phenomenon in which an individual's sense of identity and self goes beyond his/her assumed human potential. This concept is inclusive of broader aspects of human life, mind, and spirit.

(113)   (A) The detachment of egos.

The transpersonal theory is deeply central to the detachment of egos in individuals because the theory revolves around the goal of promoting individual development beyond the self. This target is reached by promoting unity between spirituality and modern psychology.

(114)   (A) Transpersonal Psychology.

Transpersonal Psychology is the field of study that deals with the transcendent and spiritual aspects of human beings. The transpersonal theories have their roots in the concept of transpersonal psychology. It helps explain the mystical and spiritual aspects of human development and the probability of developing beyond the limitations set by one's self.

(115)   (D) William James.

William James is known to be the father of the transpersonal theory. He exploited the concept that spirituality cannot be judged by its roots in a specific religion or culture, but rather by its impacts on individuals' lives.

(116)   (A) Socialization Theory.

Socialization theory revolves around the idea that society has a considerable influence on the beliefs, actions, and behavior of all people. The theory is strongly allied with developmental psychology, which conditions that human beings need social experiences for personal development and cultural evolution.

(117)   (B) Socialization.

Socialization is a sociological term that encompasses the fields of cultures, norms, and ideologies of society. The concept involves the impact of society on individuals' lives. Socialization can produce desirable results, such as morality in society, which can, in turn, encourage socially acceptable behaviors.

(118)   (B) Social Deprivation.

Social deprivation focuses on the inability of an individual to actively take part in the community or societal life, thus being the failure of the process of socialization. Also, the process of development is hindered when individuals are unable to interact with development-stimulating environmental factors.

(119)   (B) Economic.

The Tragedy of the Commons is an economic problem causing overconsumption, underinvestment, and reduction of resources. This concept is central to the element that people neglect the societal well-being and social welfare in the pursuit of self-interest.

(120)   (A) Commons, tragedy.

The statement explains the concept of Garret Hardin's "The Tragedy of the Commons." He used the metaphor of open pasture to elaborate his point of view.

(121)   (C) Garrett Hardin.

Garrett Hardin was the creator of the idea of "The Tragedy of the Commons." He explained the concept that scarcity, rivalry in consumption, and non-excludability of a common-pool resource can result in such a tragedy. In the present era, people are more self-interested and demanding more resources, which mostly exceeds supply limitations. They do not care if all the societal members have access to those scarce resources.

(122)   (C) Psychodynamic Theory.

According to the psychodynamic theory, a blend of conscious and unconscious psychological progressions influences human thoughts and conduct. Social work based on psychodynamic theory focuses on how internal emotions and processes impact individuals' personalities.

(123)   (A) Sigmund Freud.

Sigmund Freud presented the effective psychoanalytical therapy. Sigmund's ideas were new and logical as nobody before had held importance on childhood experiences. Sigmund was of the view that childhood traumas and experiences played a significant role in shaping the individuals' personalities.

(124)   (C) Psychodynamic Theory.

The psychodynamic theory conditions that human beings describe their behaviors and experiences deceptively. Their conscious mental ability works in a way to hide their true motivations and incentives. However, this does show that they are intentionally lying. Instead, this situation is related to the conscious and unconscious mind, and even humans are unable to understand.

(125)   (C) Sigmund Freud.

Sigmund Freud's impactful ideas resulted in the formation of the mind model. According to this model, three distinct layers form the human mind. Each layer is associated with a discrete set of functions and motives. For instance, the unconscious sector relates to all the primitive motivations and acts as a source for all events that recruit human behaviors.

(126)   (B) The preconscious or the subconscious.

In the context of Sigmund Freud's mind model, the preconscious or subconscious sector of the human mind is the storehouse of all memories.

(127)   (B) The id, the ego, and the superego.

After explaining the division of the human mind into three layers of the conscious, the subconscious and the unconscious, Sigmund Freud presented a structural mind model. The division of this model is based on the segments of the id, the ego, and the superego.

(128)   (A) The id.

The id sector of the human mind is the warehouse of all human motivations, desires, and primitive incentives. This segment is associated with the unconscious mind, and impulsive instincts form the id of the human mind. The id functions without the influence of the external world, and thus does not change with time or experience. Reality has no impact on the id as it works within the unconscious part of the mind.

(129)   (C) Survival and death instincts.

The id sector of the human mind includes two main drives. One of these drives is associated with the instinct of survival, and aids individuals to take part in activities that sustain life. The other drive is related to the death instincts, which motivates individuals towards dangerous and violent behaviors.

(130)   (A) The ego.

The ego of an individual functions to meet the prerequisites of the id in a socially acceptable way. According to Sigmund Freud, the ego is the modified fragment of the id and is directly influenced by the external world. The ego works by reason, unlike the id that is unreasonable and unrealistic. The decision-making part of the human mind is the ego.

(131)   (B) Superego.

The superego of the human mind motivates individuals to perform in morally acceptable ways as it is related to their sense of principle and morality. The superego holds control over the impulses of the id, such as sex and aggression, and influences the ego to transform realistic goals to moralistic goals.

(132)   (B) Childhood.

Sigmund Freud's psychoanalytical therapy is based on the element that childhood experiences, traumas, and understandings are highly influential on the personality building of an individual. The technique is useful to help vulnerable children and adolescents suffering from various issues such as mental ailments, social depression, and anxiety.

(133)   (A) Psychoanalytic.

Social work incorporating psychoanalytical approaches focuses on helping individuals to unveil their past traumas and experiences. This approach is helpful to understand the cause of the individuals' behaviors and, to make them effectively deal with these conditions so that they can evolve into better versions of themselves.

(134)   (B) Anxiety.

A proper balance of the id, the ego, and the superego segments of the human mind supports an ideal human personality. Imbalance may occur due to conflict between these elements as each is individually and powerfully influential on the human personality. This imbalance can occur if an individual has an overly dominant id, and they might become impulsive and uncontrollable as they do not weigh their acts on them being right, acceptable, or legal. On the contrary, an individual with a very dominant superego will be highly judgmental and critical as he/she may be unable to accept anything or anyone that seems immoral according to his/her ideals. To sum up, such imbalances contribute to the creation of mental disturbances such as anxiety and depression.

(135)   (A) Consciousness.

The core of consciousness is the transpersonal self; the transpersonal self is a pure self-awareness that reveals on diverse levels.

(136)   (B) Task-Centred Practice.

Task-centered practice emphasizes on reaching attainable and specific goals. The sessions for these are relatively brief, and the clients involved can vary from individuals to groups. The practicality of this model is supported with over 40 years of research; hence it is referred to as social activism's oldest 'evidence-based practice.'

(137)   (A) Client-worker collaboratively establishing attainable objectives to counter the problem.

Task-Centred Practice (TCP) involves the social worker and the client working jointly by setting measurable and attainable objectives that are achieved by setting tasks to resolve a problem.

(138)   (A) Client's preferences.

TCP entails direct involvement of the client and caters to their inclinations. Social workers must question clients about aspects they would mainly want to focus on in the process of addressing the problem. Personal preferences are considered along with a client's strength to establish a framework for the TCP model.

(139)   (C) Assessing whether or not goals are being accomplished.

TCP's substructure consists of phases that involve the advancement of the client transitioning from one phase to the next while achieving the objectives (previously set in phase one) in between. The final phase calls for analyzing the effectiveness of the response made towards the problem, which will depict whether or not to initiate a new process of TCP in case the process was not as successful as anticipated.

(140)   (B) Collectively being able to respond to challenges that could have impacts worldwide.

The field of social activism continues to expand with the additional amount of research and resources plowed into it. It has now reached a global scale that preaches the enlightenment and practicality of this profession. Globalization of social activism has paved ways for international higher authorities to come together in the case of a world emergency, to protect communities and take immediate action if need be.

(141)   (D) Economic Production, distribution, and consumption.

Globalization depicts the international cooperation of all processes that are closely related to economic development, inclusive of production, distribution, and consumption. Transactional economic organizations such as the World Bank and IMF cater to globalization requirements.

(142)   (D) Common international culture and collective global awareness

While globalization is strongly inclined towards economic aspects, in terms of a philanthropic perspective, it signifies the integration of diversity, economies, cultural differences, and political processes all dealt with justice and equality. A common international culture is emphasized in addition to a collective global awareness that indicates the externalization and implication of social work as a worldwide acknowledged profession.

(143)   (A) Local, national, and international.

In the field of social activism, responding to global matters essentially calls for three distinct scales that measure the magnitude and intensity of the crisis that needs to be addressed, all of which are looked at from different perspectives and countered accordingly.

(144)   (C) European Union.

In the hypothetical situation of a region having to face a large-scale crisis like developmental issues, regional-based political and economic unions would have to deal with the issue and take necessary measures and precautions to resolve the problem. It would call for involvement from regional and local heads of states and communities.

(145)   (C) Provision of experienced volunteers that practice welfare-improvement methods while they interact within the community.

IFRC aims at reaching its objectives by primarily supporting communities with its expert network of volunteers who are committed to practicing community-orientated approaches, while working for the well-being of the same community.

(146)   (B) While there have been several improvements in global healthcare, reaching primary objectives at the community-level remains a challenge.

Despite an increase in healthcare quality and quantity, several fundamental challenges at the community-level still exist today and are backed by recent statistics to support this fact.

(147)   (D) Expansion of primary healthcare services, improvement of healthcare, and constructive action on several aspects linked to good health.

IFRC services are based on expanding healthcare services to all communities in need, improving health care and its facilitation services, and aiming at positive action to redefine aspects closely linked to good health.

(148)   (B) Mezzo and Macro Level.

Despite IFRC's three primary objectives, it also works towards the combination of community-oriented health programs and advocates for various human rights. To increase the effectiveness in achieving these objectives, IFRC often tends to collaborate with partners at a mezzo and macro level to bring about a significant change in the communities depicting an ideal example of international integration.

(149)   (A) Global tuberculosis eradication initiative.

The great alliances between IFRC and other global organizations all aim towards a common goal of facilitating communities. These partnerships leading initiatives are practical pieces of evidence that depict the success of international integration.

(150)   (A) International Federation of Social Workers

The IFSW was founded in the late 1920s and is a part of the three primary social work organizations. The main goal of IFSW stands at promoting social work as a profession that maintains its standards and a code of ethics.

# Test 3: Questions

(1) As a social worker, what services would you be inclined to provide?

(A)Building communities, campaign on behalf of the government, and developing education services.

(B)Building mentally-healthy communities, developing health and education services, and the formation of social policies.

(C)Providing first aid and developing the healthcare sector.

(D)Campaign on behalf of the government, voluntary visits, and building communities.


(2) Social workers contribute to what nature of the services?

(A)Tangible.

(B)Intangible.

(C)Compassionate.

(D)Meaningful.


(3) Different social workers tend to specialize in diverse disciplines, which can be categorized as:

(A)Public health and medical, mental health and substance abuse, and political activism.

(B)Family children and school, political activism, fundraising, and voluntary services.

(C)Mental health and substance abuse, domestic violence, health care, and education.

(D)Family, children and school, public health and medical, mental health, and substance abuse.

(4) According to an analysis by the bureau of labor statistics, what category of social service is the most common for social workers?

(A) Family, children, and school social workers.

(B) Public health and medical social workers.

(C) Mental health and substance abuse social workers.

(D) Fundraising and voluntary service social workers.

(5) In this sector, what demand is rapidly growing?

(A) Family, children, and school social workers.

(B) Awareness.

(C) Public health workers.

(D) Non-Governmental Organizations (NGOs).

(6) Fact Check: An employment setting that involves occasional, geographical repositioning of social workers requires individuals to remain stagnant in their locations.

(A) Yes.

(B) No.

(C) Maybe.

(D) None of the above.

(7) Fact Check: Regardless of a social worker being licensed or not, they are not legally permitted to work independently catering to private clients.

(A) Yes, they are not allowed.

(B) No, only licensed workers may have their private practice and setting.

(C) No, unlicensed workers may have their private practice and setting.

(D) It is legally permissible for any social worker to work in a private or public setting independently.

(8) When did the concept of social worker's philanthropic movements come about?

(A) In the Middle Ages, dating back to the 19th century.

(B) In the Middle Ages, dating back to the 17th century.

(C) In the high middle ages, dating back to 12th century

(D) At an early age, dating back to the 14th century.

(9) Who created the poverty relief social policies?

(A) English poverty relief laws.

(B) British charity organization society (CSO).

(C) World poverty relief organization (PRO).

(D) English poor laws.

(10)    What are the three aspects from where the base of the social work profession arises?

(A) Addressing substance abuse, healthcare development policies, and socio-political actions addressing injustice.

(B) Poverty relief social policies, healthcare development policies, and settlement of injustice.

(C) Casework method, poverty relief social policies, and socio-political actions addressing injustice.

(D) Socio-economic reforms, casework method, and poverty relief development policies.

(11)    In which areas did the industrial revolution make great leaps?

(A) Scientific and technological developments.

(B) Technological developments and moral obligation.

(C) Community services and socio-economic developments.

(D) Scientific and socio-political developments.

(12)    What happened when urbanization took place in the western world in the 18th century?

(A) A surge in social problems that required more social activism.

(B) Increase in the pollution that required population control policies.

(C) The act of social activism was abolished by higher authorities and was again controlled by religious establishments.

(D) A surge in social activists that improved the state of society.

(13)    What significant historical event resulted in the ban of slavery in the United States?

(A) American Revolutionary War.

(B) World War II.

(C) Spanish-American War.

(D) American Civil War.

(14)    What did the US government do when basic amenities were needed after millions of slaves were released?

(A) Sought foreign funding and aid.

(B) Launched a public health organization.

(C) Established a social service program.

(D) Provide necessities to the public through rationing.

(15)    Which French philosopher "coined" the word 'altruism'?

(A) Auguste Comte.

(B) Jean-Paul Sartre.

(C) Voltaire.

(D) Peter Abelard.

(16)   What subject helps in distinguishing between what is right and what is wrong?

(A) Social Work.

(B) Morality.

(C) Humanitarian values.

(D) Religion.


(17)   What activities can altruism help establish that are intended to raise social welfare?

(A) Encompass the macro continuum.

(B) Building a good society.

(C) Social solidarity.

(D) Public service.


(18)   What is morality related to in many cultural systems?

(A) Social welfare and justice.

(B) Kindness and selflessness.

(C) Philanthropy and charity.

(D) Altruism and social solidarity.

(19)  What can lead to the formation of thriving communities which consider every member of the society as their responsibility?

(A) Incorporating altruistic values in an individual's life.

(B) Eradicating injustice.

(C) Holding charitable events and social services.

(D) Protest against unreasonable social policies.


(20)  What does micro to macro continuum of activities and services mean?

(A) All minor and major social services.

(B) All kinds of small and significant charitable events.

(C) It includes services related to individuals, groups, organizations, and the whole world.

(D) Services related to close friends and family.


(21)  A lack of which activities can cause societies to potentially spiral into disaster?

(A) Altruistic.

(B) Social.

(C) Individual.

(D) Organizational.

(22)    What is the definition of 'service'?

(A) To earn money through doing work for others.

(B) It is a profession that includes helping others.

(C) Helping others for free.

(D) The action of helping or doing work for someone.


(23)    What is objectivity?

(A) Being kind to everyone, regardless of their background.

(B) Being impartial in all professional activities.

(C) Helping people gain jobs.

(D) Helping people gain more resources.


(24)    What is the false self of individuals?

(A) Spontaneous, driven, and authentic.

(B) Spiritual and transcendent.

(C) A defensive and detached façade.

(D) Their behavioral aspects.


(25)    Looking out for subtleties like the client's expressions, gestures, and tone requires which of the following qualities from social workers?

(A) Emotional Intelligence.

(B) Compassion.

(C) Competitiveness.

(D) Objectivity.

(26)    From the options listed below, name the levels pertaining to the following in the correct order? Individuals and families, small groups and institutions, the community.

(A) Macro-level, micro-level, mezzo-level.

(B) Micro-level, macro-level, mezzo-level.

(C) Mezzo-level, micro-level, macro-level.

(D) Micro-level, mezzo-level, macro-level.


(27)    Name the situation in which social workers work to strike a balance between the needs of the client and the community at large?

(A) Mutual goods.

(B) Discrimination.

(C) Burnout.

(D) Secondary trauma.


(28)    Which of the following are formal professional development activities?

(A) Networking.

(B) Taking academic courses.

(C) Reading literature.

(D) Listening to podcasts.

(29)  What should social workers, who are suffering from burnout or secondary trauma, do?

(A) Quit their job.

(B) Terminate their services to the client who is putting pressure on them.

(C) Engage in self-care activities.

(D) Change their professional field.

(30)  The decline in the quality of social work in the 1980s was due to which of the following reasons?

(A) People thought social work was purely subjective.

(B) Social workers were not paid adequately.

(C) There was a rise in the crime rate.

(D) Social workers began to establish personal relationships with their clients.

(31)  What involves the shifting of the client's feelings and experiences to the social worker?

(A) Objectivity.

(B) Secondary Trauma.

(C) Emotional intelligence.

(D) Transference.

(32)    What is Making all professional decisions by submitting to evidence is called?

(A) Inclusivity.

(B) Diversity.

(C) Objectivity.

(D) Subjectivity.

(33)    What should you do to maintain strong relations with existing connections alongside your new connections?

(A) Plan parties together.

(B) Make small gestures.

(C) Invite all new and existing friends to dinner.

(D) Go with the flow.

(34)    What kind of activities can you plan with your friends and family to maintain connections and relax from a busy schedule?

(A) Organize events and parties at home.

(B) Join the gym or clubs together.

(C) Plan road trips or other meaningful experiences.

(D) All of the above.

(35)   What can help you grow and improve your existing relationship?

(A) Mutual interests and hobbies.

(B) Sharing and empathizing.

(C) Open communication and honesty.

(D) Strength and stability.

(36)   What can help other people in getting to know you better and strengthen the relationship?

(A) Doing activities together.

(B) Working out together.

(C) Sharing feelings that make you vulnerable.

(D) Remembering important events.

(37)   Which of the following is the best way to maintain your connection with friends/partners?

(A) Checking in with your friends or partner.

(B) Going to the gym together.

(C) Hangout more.

(D) Be a good listener.

(38) In busy and stressful times, what should you do so that the relationship flourishes?

(A)Text each other every day.

(B)Go out on weekends.

(C)Appreciate and acknowledge the efforts made by friends in reaching out.

(D)Call each other often.


(39) What is crucial for your mental well-being?

(A)Making lots of friends.

(B)Connecting with people.

(C)Working out with friends.

(D)Healthy relationships.


(40) What kind of people allow others to share painful feelings without dismissing them?

(A)Sympathetic people.

(B)Supportive people.

(C)Emotional people.

(D)Straightforward people.

(41)    What can healthy relationships can contribute to?

(A) Social circle and popularity.

(B) Mental and physical well-being.

(C) Health and social status.

(D) Growth and emotional well-being.


(42)    At which events is it essential for friends to be present?

(A) Milestone-events.

(B) Family events.

(C) Business events.

(D) Important events.


(43)    Which concept covers fundamental human rights, such as education, healthcare, and equal treatment of all races?

(A) Ethics.

(B) Moral conduct.

(C) Social justice.

(D) Equal treatment.

(44)    When can the concept of providing basic human rights in any society can be dated back to?

(A) 1780s.

(B) 1800s.

(C) 1790s.

(D) 1850s.


(45)    What does the concept of basic human rights teach us?

(A) Every individual is entitled to live the way they want despite society's norms.

(B) The moral entitlement of basic rights based on the norms and values of a society provided to every individual.

(C) The protection of the values and beliefs of different individuals living in a society.

(D) The right to live freely within a society by following one's own beliefs and practices.


(46)    What should be strictly prohibited to live in a fair and just society?

(A) Ethnic minorities.

(B) Differences.

(C) Acceptance of diversity.

(D) Racial discrimination.

(47)     What factors cover the principle of Access under Social Justice?

(A) Norms and regulations.

(B) Values and beliefs.

(C) Morals.

(D) Religion, race, and gender.

(48)     What is meant by 'Participation' in terms of social justice?

(A) Freedom of speech and opinion.

(B) Power of decision making for society.

(C) Involvement in all activities on the affairs of a society or community.

(D) The right to be a part of political events.

(49)     What notion is defined as the provision of services or resources to a particular segment of a society to ensure equality?

(A) Freedom.

(B) Charity.

(C) Equity.

(D) Division.

(50)     What are the three philosophical approaches used in the context of social work?

(A) Utilitarian.

(B) Libertarian.

(C) Egalitarian.

(D) All of the above.

(51)    What is the main idea behind the theory of utilitarianism?

(A) Your benefit above everyone else's.

(B) Collective benefits for everyone over individual benefits.

(C) A collection of all individual benefits.

(D) Equal benefits for every individual.

(52)    Which of the following is true regarding the theory of libertarian?

(A) The right to own your acquired resources without being coerced into the idea of equal distribution amongst everyone.

(B) The freedom to own your resources without making any contributions to the betterment of society.

(C) The right to own and distribute the resources to the minority to bridge the gap.

(D) The right to distribute resources at free will according to your wishes, irrespective of the idea of social equality.

(53)    Supporting and fighting for civil rights is an example of which of the following theories?

(A) Utilitarian.

(B) Libertarian.

(C) Egalitarian.

(D) None of the above.

(54)    The term 'immorality' can be used to describe which of the following?

(A) Having no morals.

(B) Different values.

(C) Lack of understanding.

(D) Social injustice.


(55)    Slavery, based on the color of a person's skin, falls into which of the categories listed below?

(A) Racial discrimination.

(B) Ethical difference.

(C) Labor.

(D) Social discrimination.


(56)    What is the term used for the discrimination against older people being refused the right of employed after reaching a certain age?

(A) Racial differences.

(B) Disability.

(C) Gender biases.

(D) Ageism.

(57)    Which of the following is an example of the term 'wage gap'?

(A) Different wages for experienced and inexperienced workers.

(B) Wages paid according to the qualification of each individual.

(C) Different wages for men and women working in similar positions.

(D) Wages paid based on hours worked.


(58)    What is child labor and undermining the importance of educating women examples of?

(A) Lack of choices.

(B) Differences in social norms.

(C) Societal pressure.

(D) Social injustice.


(59)    With whom does the responsibility lie to create awareness and advocate the importance of social justice among people?

(A) The government.

(B) Social workers.

(C) Religious groups.

(D) The minorities.

(60)    From the options listed below, name a type of strategy for social justice where social workers ask their clients to help spread awareness regarding human rights and bring about a positive change in different groups or communities.

(A) Change strategy.

(B) Social work.

(C) Unified policy practice.

(D) Social changes.


(61)    Which approach is used by social workers to help and support the minorities and the most vulnerable groups against social injustice?

(A) Policy advocacy.

(B) Norms and values.

(C) Coercion policies.

(D) Support groups.


(62)    How can social workers increase social justice in society?

(A) Self-promotions.

(B) Forcing their opinions onto people.

(C) Joining advocacy groups.

(D) Networking with different groups of people.

(63)    How can individuals reduce social injustice?

(A) Political protesting.

(B) Awareness campaigns.

(C) Understanding human rights.

(D) All of the above.


(64)    Which of the following is not an example of social injustice?

(A) Child labor.

(B) Difference in morals.

(C) Underage marriages and domestic abuse.

(D) Sexual orientation.


(65)    At which level are social workers engaged with entire communities, cities, and large groups of people?

(A) Organizational.

(B) Mezzo.

(C) Macro.

(D) Institutional.


(66)    What does Macro-level social work enable workers to identify?

(A) Broader social issues and solutions.

(B) National issues and solutions.

(C) Family issues and solutions.

(D) All of the above.

(67)  Macro-level social work involves professionally guided interventions specifically designed to instigate change in which arenas?

(A) Organizational.

(B) Community.

(C) Policy.

(D) All of the above.


(68)  Dealing with significant societal issues requires effective awareness regarding which aspects of an issue?

(A) Social context and solution.

(B) Political context and potential consequences.

(C) Source and potential solutions.

(D) All of the above.


(69)  From the options listed below, which of the communities or large groups does macro-level social work include?

(A) Political, religious, and cause-driven groups.

(B) Families and neighborhoods.

(C) Therapy and self-help groups.

(D) Various charities.

(70)    What kind of various roles can macro social workers play to work towards the provision of resources and effective solutions?

(A) Research analyst.

(B) Lobbyist.

(C) Policy advocates.

(D) All of the above.


(71)    Which of the following activities are macro-level social workers not involved in?

(A) Addressing national issues.

(B) Organizing community efforts.

(C) Individual counseling and emotional support.

(D) Policy analysis.


(72)    Why are macro-level social workers involved in research and community outreach programs?

(A) To produce innovative ideas.

(B) To study human behavior.

(C) To identify various social issues.

(D) To promote new research in sociology.

(73)    Which of the following is an activity related to macro-level social work?

(A) Developing programs for marginalized groups.

(B) Providing therapy to individuals.

(C) Supporting minority families.

(D) Both A and B.


(74)    How do macro-level social workers help the disadvantaged populations in society?

(A) By providing financial support.

(B) By providing emotional support.

(C) By lobbying for changes in the legislation.

(D) By protesting for their rights.


(75)    How do social workers create awareness among masses against social issues?

(A) By making them protest.

(B) By educating them.

(C) Both A and B.

(D) None of the above.

(76)   From the options listed below, what is central to the direct practice of the social work field?

(A) Program development.

(B) Community management.

(C) Political advocacy.

(D) Macro-level social work.


(77)   From the options listed below, which are the most common examples of social work at the macro-level?

(A) Community development and management.

(B) Policy analysts and advocates.

(C) Social workers and supporters.

(D) Professors and educational activists.


(78)   Policy analysts and advocates are those social workers who are usually part of which groups that work with organizations to instigate social changes?

(A) Political parties.

(B) Social services.

(C) Interdisciplinary teams.

(D) Revolutionary teams.

(79)   When does the need for social workers arise?

(A) When there is a financial strain.

(B) When the government fails to address the problems.

(C) When policymakers make faulty policies.

(D) When vulnerable people are ignored.

(80)   Coordination with which communities/institutes are essential in the macro-level social work practice?

(A) Law firms and government institutes.

(B) Conventional support structures and interdisciplinary teams.

(C) Social agencies and human service organizations.

(D) All of the above.

(81)   Which community organizations are social workers are engaged with?

(A) Police departments and juvenile centers.

(B) Small business and offices.

(C) Therapy and self-help groups.

(D) Schools, churches, and social service groups.

(82)    Which of the following has a more extensive resource base with which social workers coordinate?

(A) Self-help groups.

(B) Community clubs.

(C) Service-oriented organizations.

(D) Volunteer organizations.

(83)    In which macro-level activities are social workers commonly involved in within the organization?

(A) Raising funds for the organization.

(B) Developing social policies and legislation.

(C) Designing ethical frameworks.

(D) All of the above.

(84)    The unique skills possessed by social workers enable them to perform which activities when collaborating with human service organizations?

(A) Teaching, counseling and supporting.

(B) Networking, developing policies, and critical thinking.

(C) Research, advocating, and protesting.

(D) All of the above.

(85)   The collaboration between which groups is significantly contributing to the development of sustainable communities around the world?

(A)Vulnerable people and social workers.

(B)Policymakers and human rights activists.

(C)Social workers and community organizations.

(D)Therapy groups and social workers.


(86)   From the options listed below, which are social workers, involved in macro-level social work, not involved in?

(A)Micro social work.

(B)Mezzo social work.

(C)One-on-one counseling.

(D)None of the above.


(87)   From the options listed below, who often engage with social workers to help them identify, rectify, see problems differently, and find better solutions in their practice?

(A)Consultants.

(B)Chiropractors.

(C)Physicians.

(D)Magicians.

(88) Besides, the duration and mode of consultation, the social worker and consultant agree on a mutual basis about which of the following?

(A) Median.

(B) Functional Area.

(C) Pecuniary matters.

(D) None of the above.

(89) Besides, specialized training in the field, what other levels of qualification is required to become a consultant?

(A) Substantial Clinical Experience.

(B) A diploma in Social Work.

(C) A Molecular Biology Degree.

(D) None of the Above.

(90) Consultative professional development of people cannot be conducted in which of the cases?

(A) Dissimilar professional backgrounds.

(B) Similar professional backgrounds.

(C) Same social circles.

(D) Same interests.

(91)  Why are Individual consultation sessions usually carried out?

(A) To meet General Outcomes.

(B) For Macro-Level projects.

(C) To meet Target Driven Learning Outcomes.

(D) None of these.

(92)  Which of these is not an advantage of the Group Consultation Procedure?

(A) They focus on individual needs only.

(B) They are cost-effective.

(C) They reduce stress and isolation.

(D) They encourage story sharing.

(93)  According to the NASW, what do you call the relationship between the supervisor and supervisee that promotes the development of responsibility, skill, knowledge, attitudes, and ethical standards in the practice of clinical social work?

(A) Direction.

(B) Coordination.

(C) Osmosis.

(D) Supervision.

(94)   Which of these is a priority for the supervision process?

(A) Accountability for Client Care.

(B) Transcending parameters.

(C) Exceeding ethical standards of the profession.

(D) None of these.


(95)   What is the status of supervision (as an activity) in the professional development of social workers?

(A) Non-essential.

(B) Mandatory.

(C) Useless.

(D) Encouraged.


(96)   Which of the following is neither a function nor a type of supervision?

(A) Passive Supervision.

(B) Administrative.

(C) Educational/Clinical.

(D) Supportive.

(97)   What kind of Supervision is required to ensure that the requirements of the organization are being met and optimum work is being performed?

(A) Supportive.

(B) Passive.

(C) Clinical/Educational.

(D) Administrative.


(98)   What kind of Supervision helps develop the necessary expertise and abilities required for sound judgment, proper clinical knowledge, and skills?

(A) Clinical.

(B) Passive.

(C) Supportive.

(D) Administrative.


(99)   Which of these supervisions helps develop attitudes essential for performing clinical tasks such as psychotherapy?

(A) Passive.

(B) Clinical.

(C) Supportive.

(D) Administrative.

(100) What kind of supervision has the added function of increasing job satisfaction and reducing work-related stress?

(A) Clinical.

(B) Passive.

(C) Supportive.

(D) Administrative.


(101) Which of these is a characteristic of the social work discipline?

(A) It is narrow in its scope.

(B) It does not vary with the nature of tasks.

(C) It does not vary with the nature of the organization.

(D) It is extensive in its scope.


(102) Organizations don't entertain which of the following social workers?

(A) Incapable of achieving their objectives.

(B) Efficient.

(C) Sentimental.

(D) Dispassionate.


(103) Which of the following are not eligible to join most social work organizations?

(A) Students.

(B) Practicing professionals.

(C) Experienced social workers.

(D) None of the above.

(104)   Which of these is not an acceptable way to connect with an organization?

(A) Visit their Website.

(B) Leave a Message.

(C) Connect via Email or Cell.

(D) None of these.

(105)   What is the term for a licensed, trained, and qualified clinical social who assists individuals in coping with challenges of mental health and everyday life problems?

(A) Psychotherapist.

(B) Chiropractor.

(C) Lawyer.

(D) Archaeologist.

(106)   Along with a Master's Degree in Social Work, which of the following subjects should a social worker have studied?

(A) Individual Psychology and Mental Health.

(B) Economics.

(C) World History.

(D) Quantum Mechanics.

(107)  What, according to Karl Marx's conflict theory, is there an unequal distribution of?

(A) Resources.

(B) Power.

(C) Food.

(D) Energy.


(108)  Based on the conflict theory, what do social workers view social change as?

(A) Fictional and unreal, as power has always remained a source to influence oppression and authority.

(B) The structural formation of a class-free society.

(C) The power exchange between the dominant and the oppressed.

(D) Stability of a society.


(109)  X is the owner of a manufacturing company, employing about fifty persons. The company has three warehouses and about ten loading trucks. What are the warehouses and loading trucks example of?

(A) Bourgeoisie status.

(B) Means of production.

(C) Excessive value.

(D) Social authority.

(110)  With what life stage are developmental tasks of self-assessment and skill learning associated?

(A)Infancy (birth to 18 months).

(B)Adolescence (12-18 years).

(C)School attending age (6-12 years).

(D)Toddlerhood (18 months to 3 years).


(111)  According to the systems theory, what does "homeostasis" mean?

(A)Differentiation.

(B)Input.

(C)Steady-state.

(D)Open system.


(112)  Which of the core values listed below does social work include?

(A)Social justice.

(B)Faith and integrity.

(C)Competence.

(D)All of the above.

(113)   A social worker is working in a framework where interventions are involved in systems influenced by economic, historical, and sociopolitical factors. What level of intervention is involved in this social work practice?

(A) Micro-level.

(B) Mezzo-level.

(C) Macro-level.

(D) None of these.

(114)   Who was the first psychologist to approve the concept of the transpersonal theory in social work practice?

(A) William James.

(B) Erik Erikson.

(C) Carl Jung.

(D) None of these.

(115)   Which of the following intervention techniques is not based on transpersonal theories and concepts?

(A) Meditation, mindfulness, and contemplation.

(B) Visualization, inner concentration, image-building, and dreaming.

(C) Reformed states of consciousness.

(D) Spiritual awakening, animism, an interpersonal transformation of mind and body.

(116)   Which of the following is/are the probable solutions to the tragedy of the commons?

(A) Raising tax rates for businesses.

(B) Privatization of properties.

(C) Enforcement of laws and regulations.

(D) Both (B) and (C).


(117)   Which of the following set is entirely an example of the tragedy of commons?

(A) Earthquakes and tsunamis.

(B) Excessive rainstorms and floods.

(C) Pollution and inflation.

(D) Overfishing and overgrazing.


(118)   Garrett Hardin used a metaphor to explain the concept of the tragedy of the commons. What was it?

(A) Excessive use of groundwater.

(B) Extreme mining.

(C) Overfishing.

(D) Overgrazing pasturelands.

(119)  Which of the following statements best explains the concept of the tragedy of the commons?

(A) The conflict between individual and collective responsibility.

(B) Transfer of short-term positive effects on the individual.

(C) Transfer of long-term negative effects on society.

(D) None of these.


(120)  According to Erikson's Eight Stages of Development, during which stage does the psychological phase of trust versus mistrust develop?

(A) Infancy.

(B) Toddlerhood.

(C) Young adulthood.

(D) Adolescence.


(121)  Which of the following explains Erikson's Eight Stages of Development?

(A) Psychoanalytical.

(B) Transpersonal.

(C) Psychosocial.

(D) Behavioral.

(122) According to Erik Erikson, how many stages of development are present in an individual's life?

(A)6.

(B)7.

(C)8.

(D)9.

(123) Early relationships influence later relationships. How is this possible?

(A)The prototype helps to enable the development of internal processes.

(B)Through imprinting.

(C)Through adaptation mechanisms.

(D)None of these.

(124) Why does an individual have to evolve from the trust vs. mistrust stage effectively, and why is this achievement important?

(A)Because if unsuccessful, the individual will develop anxiety and insecurity.

(B)Because if unsuccessful, the individual will not be able to understand the concept of trust.

(C)Because if unsuccessful, the individual will become trustworthy.

(D)Because if unsuccessful, the individual will grow up as a liar.

(125)  Which of the following is not one of Erikson's Eight Stages of Development?

(A) Trust versus mistrust.

(B) Intimacy versus isolation.

(C) Industry versus inferiority.

(D) Life versus death.


(126)  What is the social conflict associated with the young adulthood stage of development?

(A) Trust versus mistrust.

(B) Intimacy versus isolation.

(C) Industry versus inferiority.

(D) Integrity versus despair.


(127)  What quality appears from the eighth stage of psychosocial development?

(A) Hope.

(B) Wisdom.

(C) Will.

(D) Love and compassion.

(128) What was Erikson's theory of eight psychosocial stages that was central to the development of?

(A) Personality.

(B) Ego identity.

(C) Social psyche.

(D) Psychosocial conflict.

(129) Which of the following shows the stage of autonomy versus shame?

(A) An infant drinking milk from a feeder.

(B) A preschooler insisting on picking out food and clothes of her own choice.

(C) A middle schooler working hard to do well in school.

(D) None of these.

(130) Psychoanalytical theories are based on which concept?

(A) There is an unconscious self-realization strength within everyone.

(B) Humanity's own potential beyond the self.

(C) Human behavior is based on rationality.

(D) Humans' actions are a product of external influences.

(131) From the options listed below, which conflict is linked with middle adulthood?

(A) Industry versus inferiority.

(B) Autonomy versus shame.

(C) Both (A) and (B).

(D) Generativity versus stagnation.

(132)  What helps individuals to hold off the intimidating id impulses?

(A) Cognitive behaviors.

(B) Psychological therapies.

(C) Defense mechanisms.

(D) None of the above.


(133)  Which of the following defines id?

(A) A segment of the human psyche that controls morals.

(B) A segment of the human psyche that controls impulses.

(C) A segment of the human psyche that is the storehouse of innate needs.

(D) None of the above.


(134)  According to Sigmund Freud's mind model, which is the segment of the psyche that is associated with the learned values from the surroundings?

(A) The oral stage.

(B) The id.

(C) The ego.

(D) The superego.


(135)  What segment of the human psyche develops last?

(A) The id.

(B) The ego.

(C) The superego.

(D) None of these.

(136)  What is the main objective of The World Health Organization?

(A) Provision of free healthcare services to all of humanity.

(B) Attainment by all peoples of the highest possible level of health.

(C) Creating awareness in every aspect of health-related issues.

(D) Endorsing necessary precautions through every health crisis.


(137)  Which of the following is a primary goal of the World Health Organization?

(A) Devise healthcare policies and regulations.

(B) Provide free medical care to individuals worldwide.

(C) Create awareness campaigns for health crises.

(D) Precisely keep global health statistics in check


(138)  What does the interconnectedness of the beliefs of international social work practice depict?

(A) The emergence of common culture that is encouraged to prevail over communities.

(B) The integration of health organizations to formulate and readjust health regulations.

(C) International health authorities must work in a coalition to resolve social matters.

(D) The quality of life is directly influenced by social, political, and economic events.


(139)  What factors impact the quality of human life and human rights directly?

(A) Economic, health, and education events.

(B) Education, social and economic events.

(C) Health, education, and political events.

(D) Social, political, and economic events.

(140)   Which of the following is not a belief of international social work practice?

(A) Global North-South Divide.

(B) Social, Political, and Economic Roots.

(C) Faith in Peace.

(D) Empathic behavior.


(141)   What goal of international social work's emphasis is on dealing with systemic oppression?

(A) Eliminating barriers.

(B) Increase in healthcare services.

(C) Empathic behavior.

(D) Balanced approach.


(142)   Around goals does international social work revolve?

(A) Enhancing global development and assisting communities.

(B) Redefining social policies.

(C) Providing social justice.

(D) None of the above.

(143)  What best defines the goal of a 'balanced approach'?

(A) Counter any social problem by endorsing common culture and eliminating discrimination.

(B) To ensure client objectives are met without wasting resources.

(C) Maintaining a balance between social and economic development.

(D) The ability to convert fundamental concepts into practical approaches.


(144)  Which of the following is not a goal of international social work?

(A) Poverty elimination.

(B) Having faith in peace.

(C) Rights for all.

(D) Novel social arrangements.


(145)  Narrative therapy calls for personifying problems, to what extent is this effective?

(A) It is ineffective.

(B) It assists clients in remembering tragic past experiences.

(C) It finds an immediate solution to the problem without identifying the root.

(D) It helps the client view the problem from a different perspective as a separate entity.


(146)  Which of the following is not a technique used in solution-focused therapy?

(A) Seven-stage crisis.

(B) Exception-finding.

(C) Scaling and miracle questions.

(D) Relationship questions.

(147) What word best describes the realistic timeframe given to clients to achieve objectives for a task-centered practice model?

(A) Concise.

(B) Lengthy.

(C) Discursive.

(D) None of the above.

(148) Can the phases that are applied over clients in TCP be easily overlapped?

(A) Yes.

(B) It depends on the ability of the worker.

(C) No.

(D) Phases do not exist in TCP.

(149) To avoid environmental degradation in globalization, what kind of subjective understanding must a social worker possess?

(A) Diversification of cultural values and lives.

(B) Awareness of healthcare crises.

(C) Factors adversely affecting the environmental well-being.

(D) Importance of international integration among organizations.

(150) Why are IFRC's international integration and collaborations important?

(A) Increase in healthcare provision for minority communities.

(B) It establishes the concept of peace worldwide.

(C) It helps to stabilize the economy in countries with a higher population of underprivileged.

(D) Assistance to counter any global issues that may arise as a result of crises that affect humanity.

# Test 3: Answers & Explanations

(1)  (B) Building mentally-healthy communities, developing health and education services, and the formation of social policies.

The essential traits of a social worker involve strengthening communities by endorsing psychotherapy and counseling, work for the progression of the healthcare and education sector, and provide assistance in social policy formation.

(2)  (A) Tangible.

As a social worker, a duty to provide tangible services to people who seek or require assistance must be fulfilled. Their substantial services include consistently developing healthcare sectors and working for the progression of education systems. Communities are strengthened by an emphasis on mental health, with the help of counseling. Creating, rewriting, and encouraging the implementation of social policies are extended forms of the attributes of social workers.

(3)  (D) Family, Children and School, Public Health and Medical, Mental Health, and substance abuse.

Social workers all work differently to reach divergent objectives and goals. The social issues may be tackled with several outlooks, including psychological, social, individual, or political angles. From a broader perspective, the expertise offered by social workers in various domains falls into three categories, namely; Family, Children and School, Public Health and Medical, Mental Health, and substance abuse. Each consists of a specialized department of social activism dedicated to altering community circumstances for the better.

(4) (A) Family children and school social workers.

Family, children, and school social workers primarily aid students and families by interacting with schools and settling down any uncalled-for matters. Working with the school and instructors to, for instance, cater to a child's learning disabilities are a significant factor that needs to be dealt with by activists working in this domain. Such social workers are the most common around the world, which would explain the higher degree of activists involved in this genre.

(5) (C) Public health workers.

Activists who are a part of the public healthcare system are the second most common welfare group of social workers. With rising health concerns, the dire need for more health-based workers is essential to cater to healthcare crises. The situation is similar to the current on-going crisis and pandemic, where NGOs, federal, and local body governments are consistently urging individuals to volunteer for the healthcare sector in their country

(6) (C) Maybe.

Social workers specializing in different domains would need to cater to various needs relevant to the category in which they opted to work. Geographical mobilization differs based on the perspective or approach the activist is adopting to tackle a situation, as well as the nature of the chosen setting.

(7) (B) No, only licensed workers may have their private practice and setting.

Generally, social workers that are licensed and registered with an association, and possess relevant experience in dealing within the public welfare domain in which they are opting to work, may choose to work under a private setting while independently catering to clients. The rising demand for social workers in countries tends to ease restrictions. However, the requirements of a licensed worker may differ from one country's policy to another.

(8) (A) In the Middle Ages, dating back to the 19th century.

Social justice and philanthropic movements arose from church-based ministering in the middle age of the 19th century, previously dedicated to the betterment of the needy in society. The practice remains alive and consistent today as it is deeply embedded into these and other similar movements.

(9) (D) English Poor Laws.

The social work profession can be subcategorized and looked upon from three distinct perspectives. One of these was created back in the 17th century by the English Poor Laws that formed poverty relief social policies dedicated to improving the well-being of the less fortunate.

(10) (C) Casework method, poverty relief social policies, and socio-political actions addressing injustice.

The social work foundation aspects were created by different organizations, three of which were relatively prominent. Namely, the poverty relief social policies by the English Poor Laws in the 17th century, British Charity Organization (CSO)'s casework method in the 19th century, and socio-political actions that are inclined towards serving social justice from the house settlement movement.

(11) (A) Scientific and technological developments.

Urbanization of societies resulted in formal social welfare organizations taking over the domain of humanitarian assistance from religious establishments. It was mainly due to the awareness that arose among people, with the technological and scientific developments of society that ultimately lead to modernization.

(12)    (A) A surge in social problems that required more social activism.

With more urbanization, social problems grew significantly, and social workers were most needed to tackle circumstances. Newer humanitarian- aid methods were discovered to address social issues such as poverty and mental illness.

(13)    (D) American Civil War.

The emphasis on how prevalent injustice was in society was made quite evident after the historical events of the American Civil War, which ultimately led to the prohibition of slavery in the United States. A myriad of unfortunate consequences that had to be dealt with, as a result of the war.

(14)    (C) Established a social service program.

The US government launched a social service program after the country experienced a surge in welfare problems that resulted in the displacement of families, which were dealt with along with the homeless and unemployed.

(15)    (A) Auguste Comte.

The French philosopher coined the word altruism back in the 19th century and used it to describe a person's moral obligation to devote themselves to the service of people.

(16)    (B) Morality.

Morality helps an individual understand the difference between good and evil. It gives a sense of judgment to a person that is based on firmly distinguishing between right and wrong.

(17)    (C) Social solidarity.

Altruism, in a broad sense, consists of such activities that automatically brings the society closer. Altruism is one of the main factors of building a good society that requires universal solidarity, communal cooperation, and selflessness.

(18)    (D) Altruism and social solidarity.

Even though almost all cultural systems are based on promoting the welfare of others and cooperation among society, but altruism and social solidarity are such aspects that are closely related to mortality. Among all others, altruism and social solidarity play a more prominent role in functioning society.

(19)    (A) Incorporating altruistic values in an individual's life.

The ultimate goal of social work is social welfare, which is induced through altruism. Without the effects of altruistic values in individuals' lives, a society cannot practice social work and social solidarity.

(20)    (C) It includes services related to individuals, groups, organizations, and the whole world.

Social solidarity, social welfare, and social services are all essential steppingstones for building a better functioning society. However, their effects are not limited to only individuals, but they can also lead to positive changes on a global level.

(21)    (A) Altruistic.

Altruism presents the concept of considering the needs of others above your own. The activities related to altruism further gives life to social welfare, organization, and individual activities for the benefit of society and its people.

(22)    (D) The action of helping or doing work for someone.

Service is the basic foundation of social work where people volunteer to provide services to those in need. Their desire to provide services is based on the motivation of doing much more than just a job.

(23)    (B) Being impartial in all professional activities.

Objectivity is a philosophical concept which involves being completely independent of subjectivity created by emotions, perception, or imagination. It is often associated with traits such as impartiality, detachment, and submission to evidence. Objectivity is an important principle to maintain in every profession, including social work.

(24)    (C) A defensive and detached façade.

Self-awareness is essential to discharge the role of the self. Psychological studies suggest that many individuals detach themselves from their true selves and attribute their individuality to their false selves. The true self is meant to be authentic, driven, and spontaneous. The false self, on the other hand, is believed to be a defensive façade that leaves its holders feeling dispassionate and uncompassionate. It is a manifestation of what people think the society expects them to be rather than what they are.

(25)    (A) Emotional Intelligence.

Social workers usually work in environments where they have to be particularly observant of subtle gestures, expressions, and behavioral aspects of their clients to diagnose their problem areas and suggest solutions. Looking out for subtleties requires emotional astuteness and intelligence, which a social worker can only acquire if they are aware of the subtleties of their own emotions.

(26)    (D) Micro-level, mezzo-level, macro-level.

In social work, individuals and families consist of the micro-level. Small groups and institutions are at the mezzo-level while the community is considered to be at the macro-level of social work, which is the highest level in the field.

(27)    (A) Mutual goods.

Social workers are mindful of their responsibility for the mutual goods problem. In this problem, they work to strike a balance between the needs of the client and the community at large. The concept of egalitarianism helps them realize this responsibility and solve the problem.

(28)   (B) Taking academic courses.

Professional development activities can be formal or informal. Formal activities include enrolling in university courses, attending seminars and workshops, taking online courses, attending conferences and workshops, participating in discussion groups, webinars, and can also include on the job training. On the other hand, informal activities include reading books and literature, engaging in networking activities, and developing advocacy networks.

(29)   (C) Engage in self-care activities.

Burnout and secondary trauma occur due to exhaustion and pressure from the work. Since social work is a labor-intensive job, it can take a toll on the wellbeing of social workers. Hence, social workers must devote some time to themselves and engage in self-help activities, which help them navigate through the pressures of their job in a healthy way. It helps them maintain a balance between their professional and personal lives. Otherwise, they turn to unhealthy coping mechanisms that affect their job negatively.

(30)   (A) People thought social work was purely subjective.

In the postmodernism era, many people critiqued the social work profession because they thought it was very subjective and was only involved with subjective causes. There was a considerable rise in skepticism amongst people regarding the professional field.

(31)   (D) Transference.

In the field of psychology, transference is when a client redirects or projects their feelings from an important person in their life (a significant other or a close relation) to the clinician. It is a useful concept to project into social work. This process is often done unconsciously and is more likely to happen in a therapeutic setting where the person who is undergoing the therapy may apply his feelings or emotions towards the therapist.

(32)    (C) Objectivity.

Objectivity involves making decisions without your emotions or personal opinions affecting the decision. Objective professionals only make decisions based on the evidence and data provided to them.


(33)    (B) Make small gestures.

Making new connections doesn't mean the existing ones have lost their value. However, one must make small gestures now and then remind them they are still relevant. You can plan parties, road trips, and other activities, but these are not always possible. What you can do anytime is to make small gestures and simple acts like bringing flowers, doing chores, watching a movie, or eating together because these acts make you feel loved.


(34)    (D) All of the above.

There are loads of activities you can plan to freshen up your existing relationships with something as simple as just talking or something as exciting as going on a road trip. Planning fitness activities together, going out to bond, or just taking a break from your busy schedule.


(35)    (C) Open communication and honesty.

Any relationship, whether new or existing, needs a high level of open communication that is based on complete honesty. These are integral factors that help improve bonds. Being a good listener and an attentive person will nurture your relationship.


(36)    (C) Sharing feelings that make you vulnerable.

Discussing your fears, weaknesses, and insecurities with your friends builds a secure connection. It allows people to understand you more and strengthens the relationship.

(37)   (A) Checking in with your friends or partner.

In today's busy life, it is hard to meet people every day. So, one of the best ways to maintain a connection with people is to check in on them now and then. You can call them and ask follow-up questions and make meaningful conversation.

(38)   (C) Appreciate and acknowledge the efforts made by friends in reaching out.

It is often hard to make time every day within our busy schedules. However, when friends try to reach out, you should acknowledge their efforts and appreciate them connecting with you. Expressing gratitude is an essential factor in relationships.

(39)   (D) Healthy relationships.

A healthy relationship brings peace and calm into your life. A relationship where there is no mutual respect, honesty, or healthy boundaries, can become incredibly frustrating. That is why it is crucial to maintain healthy relationships with friends/partners.

(40)   (B) Supportive people.

Support in a relationship strengthens the bond between people. A supportive relationship allows people to express concern without the fear of being judged. Supportive people give others the confidence to share difficult feelings without dismissing them. They are trustworthy and honest people.

(41)   (D) Growth and emotional well-being.

Meaningful connections with people allow healthy relationships to nurture. These kinds of relationships promote growth and improve your emotional well-being.

(42)   (A) Milestone-events.

True friends are not only present in difficult times, but they must be present at every milestone-event, including birthdays, promotions, important family events, and other supportive events.

(43)    (C) Social justice.

Social justice is the right of every human being. It covers all aspects of basic human rights that every individual must have, including foreign citizens as well as criminals. It would be highly unethical to deprive people of their basic rights and treat them differently based on their background.

(44)    (A) 1780s.

The concept of social justice dates back to the 1780s. The term 'social justice' was openly used in the 1780s; however, the idea of having basic human rights and justice was already prevalent in some parts of the world.

(45)    (B) The moral entitlement of basic rights based on the norms and values of a society provided to every individual.

Basic human rights include the right to receive a formal education, freedom of speech and thought, and the right to a fair trial for criminal justice. It is about living in a society with specific rules and regulations based on the collective interest of people's needs and rights.

(46)    (D) Racial discrimination.

People from different cultural backgrounds are present everywhere. They may live in the same place, but they have significant differences based on many factors such as race, religious beliefs, and customs. The most important element of social justice is the concept of fair and equal treatment of people from all walks of life. A person should not be treated any differently for practicing a different religion.

(47)    (D) Religion, race, and gender.

Everyone has the right to have the necessities for survival, such as food, shelter, and clothing. The basic necessities of life are not dependent on ethnicity or religion. They are not different for anyone; even criminals and outlaws have the right to have access to the basic means of living.

(48)     (A) The freedom of speech and opinion.

Social justice covers the right to express your opinions and ideas. Every individual, irrespective of what segment he or she may belong to, has the right to freedom of speech and participation. By discouraging or preventing someone from participating will lead to conflicts and discrimination.

(49)     (C) Equity.

Social equity is a way to maintain balance and equality among people of various segments. It includes the rights of minorities to have access to more resources to be on the same scale and avoid injustice.

(50)     (D) All of the above.

The three theories discuss and define ways in which societies can thrive and practice equality and social justice without discrimination. They give a new perspective on how the resources could be distributed more effectively and equally amongst every segment of society.

(51)     (B) Collective benefits for everyone over individual benefits.

The theory of Utilitarian revolves around the notion of disregarding individual rights or benefits by looking at everyone's interests and benefits at large. Any action will be considered morally correct if it is supported or accepted by the majority of people.

(52)     (A) The right to own your acquired resources without being coerced into the idea of equal distribution amongst everyone.

The theory of libertarian does not believe in the equal distribution of the resources for everyone. This theory focuses on individual autonomy over the resources that have been rightly earned. Libertarians believe that they have the freedom of choice when it comes to the sharing of these resources.

(53)    (C) Egalitarian.

This theory supports the idea of promoting and granting equal rights and the same treatment for everyone. The civil rights reject any type of political or social injustice and demand equal treatment for everyone as a moral obligation.

(54)    (D) Social injustice.

Social injustice refers to unfair treatment based on the provision of human rights or the unequal distribution of resources. It prevails in many societies and is often overlooked. It may be linked to any part of your life, even as a child. For example, child labor is prevalent in most countries.

(55)    (A) Racial discrimination.

Unfortunately, the practice of treating people differently, based on their race, is still present in most parts of the world. Racial discrimination is when a person is granted unfair treatment or is considered to have lower standards based on the color of the skin and racial background.

(56)    (D) Ageism.

Ageism is an example of discrimination against individuals belonging to the older age group in society. It prevents older people from working as they are considered to be a liability. Their contributions are considered less valuable and useful compared to those of younger individuals.

(57)    (C) Different wages for men and women working at similar positions.

Wage gaps are prevalent in many organizations. They are not only limited to gender differences as these gaps may be based on age, ethnicity, religion, and caste. It is harder for women to reach higher positions in the workplace since they are not recognized as essential or valuable employees in most organizations. However, some organizations are taking the necessary steps to reduce wage gaps and gender biases.

(58)     (D) Social injustice.

There are many forms of social injustice and discrimination, and some are considered normal and acceptable in many societies. For example, a prevalent unfair practice in most societies is unfair treatment or criminal justice for rich and poor.


(59)     (B) Social workers.

As a social worker, you must ensure that people understand their rights. Social workers are required to promote justice and equal treatment of all groups, which can be done by starting campaigns, joining advocacy groups, or attending social events related to the cause.


(60)     (C) Unified policy practice.

It is an effective way of creating awareness among people, being beneficial for the clients, and the community at large. It helps social workers connect better with their clients by assisting them throughout the process and addressing their issues.


(61)     (A) Policy advocacy.

This approach is used by social workers to encourage and promote social justice for minorities. For example, social workers could speak on behalf of a family or a group of people belonging to a different race, ensuring that they get fair treatment in all respects.


(62)     (C) Joining advocacy groups.

There are many ways in which social workers can increase the awareness of social justice. Joining an advocacy group is one such method where the social workers support human rights and actively take part in encouraging people to understand their rights and voice their opinions.

(63)    (D) All of the above.

The people living in communities can also make themselves heard by taking specific precautionary steps to fight for justice. Those who are oppressed should raise their voice and know their rights. Advocacy groups can organize peaceful political campaigns and protests to seek the attention of policymakers so that their views can be heard.

(64)    (B) Difference in morals.

Having different morals is not part of social injustice. Morals of one society or one country may be different from another. As long as morals do not contradict fundamental human rights, they are acceptable. For example, a country may consider it immoral for women to go out of a house unaccompanied by a male member of the family. While this is morally acceptable in one country, it may not be acceptable in another.

(65)    (C) Macro.

The field of social work is divided into three categories: micro, mezzo, and macro. Macro-level social work involves interactions with larger communities or major institutions. Micro and mezzo-level social work corresponds to small or an intermediate level social work.

(66)    (A) Broader social issues and solutions.

Macro-level social work addresses social issues on a much larger scale that is faced on the community level. They are usually not involved in one-on-one interactions.

(67)    (D) All of the above.

Macro practices and interventions are targeted towards issues at a much larger scale. Community problems faced by the population in a broader context are dealt with within the macro-level of social work.

(68)   (B) Political context and potential consequences.

Since macro-level social work is directly involved in dealing with social issues on a much larger scale, social workers must be knowledgeable about the potential consequences of intervening in community-level problems. People dealing with societal issues in a broader context must have an awareness of all political contexts related to the issues.

(69)   (A) Political, religious, and cause-driven groups.

Macro-level social work caters to the need of entire communities. These communities can be anything from cities and towns to large groups such as international organizations and religious communities.

(70)   (D) All of the above.

Macro social workers can take on many roles to overcome obstacles and issues faced by communities. They can play various roles in the field to tackle these mammoth problems and come up with effective solutions. Apart from being emotional supporters and one-on-one councilors, social workers can be community organizers and policy advocates.

(71)   (C) Individual counseling and emotional support.

Macro-level social workers are involved in activities related to social research work, organizational development, and community educational initiatives. Micro-level social workers are engaged in individual services and support, but macro-level social work is done on national and international levels.

(72)   (C) To identify various social issues.

One of the everyday activities for macro-level social workers includes investigating social issues that society is facing.

(73)    (A) Developing programs for marginalized groups.

Macro-level social workers take many initiatives and launch different programs to assist the most vulnerable groups and communities—these programs, in return, target specific issues like creating support programs and the provision of adequate healthcare.

(74)    (C) By lobbying for changes in the legislation.

Many macro-level social workers advocate the rights and needs of underprivileged individuals in the community. They help the disadvantaged population in society by lobbying for changes and engaging with government officials for the provision of necessities.

(75)    (B) By educating them.

One of the examples of macro-level social work is to educate people about their basic rights. Macro-level social workers are involved in various educational initiatives and activities which help teach people about existing social problems and injustice.

(76)    (D) Macro-level social work.

Macro-level social work is essential to the mission and goal of the social work field. The impact of macro-level social work improves the welfare of society through activities such as educating people, advocating for their rights, and political advocacy. However, all these activities fall under the banner of macro-level social work.

(77)    (B) Policy analysts and advocates.

Social workers encompassing these roles are directly involved in raising awareness of the social issues that negatively affect the population. They work towards developing strategies of these social issues on a large scale.

(78)    (C) Interdisciplinary teams.

Social workers who work as policy analysts at different organizations and other non-profit human rights groups are part of these interdisciplinary teams. They work with law firms, policy think tanks, and other human service organizations for legislative and social changes for the welfare of the population.


(79)    (B) When the government fails to address the problems.

When conventional support structures such as governments fail to look after the problems of the people, the need for the services of social workers arises. Social workers tend to look after the basic needs of people and formulate a system that can help sustain the change.


(80)    (C) Social agencies and human service organizations.

Organizations such as these employ social workers who help meet their goals of social welfare. Organizations such as these have the necessary resources and capabilities that help social workers use them on a larger scale.


(81)    (D) School, churches, and social service groups.

Macro-level social workers are engaged with many community organizations. These may include professional service agencies, informal groups, and voluntary organizations. Within these non-profit organizations are entities such as fraternities, schools, clubs, and healthcare units.


(82)    (C) Service-oriented organizations.

Service-oriented organizations have a more extensive resource base compared to smaller or volunteer groups. Social workers coordinate with these organizations to make use of their ample resources so that they can use them for the most beneficial activities for the society.

(83)    (D) All of the above.

The role of social workers can be at any level, from micro to macro. However, when it comes to macro-level practices within organizations, social workers are involved in all of the above activities and more. Fruitful results are achieved when such organizations and social workers collaborate for the welfare of society.

(84)    (B) Networking, developing policies, and critical thinking.

Social workers have many unique skills that they offer to human service organizations to take stances on behalf of the vulnerable population. They engage themselves in beneficial activities such as research, critical thinking, counseling, and networking to promote the values and principles of the field of social work.

(85)    (C) Social workers and community organizations.

The collaboration between community organizations and social workers is incredibly important. These collaborations help in solving different issues in society and work hand in hand to propagate the human cause.

(86)    (D) None of the above.

Social workers involved in macro-level social work need to be engaged in micro or mezzo-level social work. Social workers can be involved in any level of activities that promote the welfare of society.

(87)    (A) Consultants

The consultant often engages social workers to help identify and correct any mistakes in their practice. They may help them look at a problem differently and find better solutions. Consultants also impart knowledge to polish the skills of new social workers.

(88)    (B) Functional Area.

The social worker and consultant agree on a mutual basis about the duration of consultation, the mode, and the functional area that needs to be the primary domain of discussion. Social workers should seek clinical consultation from a member practicing the same profession.

(89)    (A) Substantial Clinical Experience.

Besides substantial training in the field, a consultant –to function properly in their capacity – must possess substantial clinical experience. They can then use this experience to tackle challenges, both traditional and novel, and better assist social workers.

(90)    (A) Dissimilar Professional backgrounds.

Professional development through consultation is usually conducted on a one-on-one basis, in groups, or with people from similar backgrounds and social circles. When people are from dissimilar professional backgrounds, they are at different levels of understanding, and it is harder to take everyone through the consultation process together. A consultation session with people from the same professional background who share a similar level of proficiency and knowledge is better suited to support and encourage one another.

(91)    (C) To meet Target Driven Learning Outcomes.

Individual sessions are carried out to meet specific target driven learning outcomes. They usually last for about an hour, but this may be subject to change as per the agreement.

(92)    (A) They Focus on Individual Needs only

Group sessions focus on a particular group to address the training needs of the social workers together (not individual needs). Social workers have the advantage of learning from one another's experiences as well as from the consultant's skills and practices. It helps reduce the level of stress and isolation as you get to share stories about how you overcame particular challenges and how you are dealing with different situations. Group sessions save time and are cost-effective.

(93)    (D) Supervision.

According to NASW, "Supervision is the relationship between the supervisor and supervisee that promotes the development of responsibility, skill, knowledge, attitudes, and ethical standards in the practice of clinical social work. The priority of the supervision process is accountability for client care within the parameters and ethical standards of the social work profession."

(94)    (A) Accountability for Client Care.

The priority of the supervision process is accountability for client care within the parameters and ethical standards of the social work profession."

(95)    (B) Mandatory.

Supervision is considered a mandatory activity for the professional development of social workers. The social worker is informed about their mistakes as they work and learn from their mentors.

(96)    (A) Passive supervision

There is no mode of supervision known as "Passive Supervision." Supportive, Clinical/Educational and Administrative are the known supervision modes.

(97)   (D) Administrative.

Administrative supervision is required to ensure that the requirements of the organization are being met and optimum work is being performed.

(98)   (A) Clinical.

Clinical supervision develops the expertise and abilities required for sound judgment, proper clinical knowledge, and skills, including self-reflection. Clinical supervision helps social workers understand the code of ethics and values, and it hones the learning capacity of an individual.

(99)   (B) Clinical.

Clinical supervision develops the expertise, abilities, and attitudes needed for performing clinical tasks such as psychotherapy. Clinical supervision helps social workers understand the code of ethics and values, and it hones the learning capacity of an individual.

(100)   (C) Supportive.

Supportive supervision is used to improve the morale of social workers by providing encouragement and support. It is not much different from administrative or clinical supervision, but it has the added function of increasing job satisfaction and reducing work-related stress.

(101)   (D) It is extensive in its scope.

The social work profession is vast and varies according to the type of task and nature of the organization. Social workers possess the skills to advocate their knowledge effectively and positively influence organizations. For example, a clinical social worker has command over the subject and will easily be able to preach to organizations about the importance of self-reflection or self-awareness.

(102)   (A) Incapable of Achieving their Objectives.

Organizations don't usually entertain social workers who are not proficient with or capable of doing what they set out to achieve. How a social worker informs and influences an organization is different for each individual as everyone has a different capacity for learning.

(103)   (D) None of the Above.

The members eligible to join the organization may include students, practicing professionals, and experienced clinical social workers. All of these play important roles in social work organizations within their capacities.

(104)   (D) None of these.

There are usually ways in which you can connect with organizations. You could visit their website and leave a message or connect with them via email or telephone. It all starts with small steps, and you gradually work your way to the top.

(105)   (A) Psychotherapist.

A licensed clinical social worker is a trained and qualified psychotherapist who assists individuals in coping with the challenges. Their overall function is to improve the quality of life and help people find their way out of social and mental issues.

(106)   (A) Individual Psychology and Mental Health.

A qualified social worker needs to possess some sort of relevant academic background, and this allows workers to fundamentally comprehend issues that arise and then use their expertise and experience to cater to it and practically apply the knowledge they have over the issue itself. Social workers need to have studied sociology, individual psychology, mental health theory and practice, and human behavior.

(107)  (B) Power.

Karl Marx was of the view that the power differential in a society leads to the formation of dominant and oppressed groups. The emerging dominant groups or individuals try to hold control over society through manipulation and authority. These groups uphold their self-interests at the cost of society's welfares, which creates several social disturbances such as injustice and oppression amongst the underprivileged inhabitants of the society.

(108)  (C) Power exchange between the dominant and the oppressed.

Karl Marx proposed in the conflict theory that the conflicts within a society are the primary source of change. That is to say that revolutions result from the power differential, i.e., the domination of one class over the other. This power conflict results in the production of deviant behavior. Karl Marx emphasized the marginalization and alienation amongst the proletariat, which, in turn, creates power differential.

(109)  (B) Means of production.

Since the warehouses and loading trucks are registered and owned by the company, they are considered a means of production.

(110)  (C) School attending age (6-12 years).

In Erikson's Eight Stages of Development, this is the stage in which children are actively learning new skills and knowledge. This stage is the most social stage of development, as in this period, the parents are no longer the only influence on the child. Instead, children get inspirations from every individual and environment they come across.

(111)  (C) Steady-state.

"Homeostasis" or "steady-state" in systems theory is the accomplishment of a balance within a family system. It is defined as the tendency towards relative stability between interdependent elements, especially as supported by psychological courses.

(112)   (D) All of the above.

The success of social work lies in the blend of specific core values. These include social justice, dignity, integrity, competence, and a sense of responsibility. Competence allows social workers to absorb knowledge, apply theoretical concepts, and make effective interventions. They must stick to the ethical principles of integrity as this helps support a strong code of behavior, honesty, trustworthiness, respect, and a sense of justice.

(113)   (C) Macro-level.

The fields of study related to systems theory categorize into micro, mezzo, and macro levels. At the micro-level, individual relationships and family systems are studied. The mezzo level deals with institutional and organizational impacts on individuals' lives. And finally, the macro level, society-wide influences such as laws and cultures are studied.

(114)   (C) Carl Jung.

William James is known to be the founder of the transpersonal theory, but Carl Jung was the first psychologist to legitimize the concept. He was of the viewpoint that consciousness itself had inherent tendencies toward growth, development, and evolution.

(115)   (D) Spiritual awakening, animism, an interpersonal transformation of mind and body.

Spiritual awakening, animism, the transformation of mind and body, and interpersonal processes are not considered to be the traditional interventional methods of psychotherapy and transcendent counseling. Mediation is the most common technique in interventions based on transcendent and spiritual therapies.

(116)　(D) Both (B) and (C).

Garrett Hardin proposed the implementation of laws and regulations and the privatization of properties as the solutions to the tragedy of the commons. These solutions were based on the element that individuals would always act upon their self-interests. That is why Hardin preferred privatization so that individuals have the incentive to manage their property and, thus, are the only ones harmed by their actions.

(117)　(D) Overfishing and overgrazing.

Both fishes and pasturelands are the "commons." Excessive and non-regulated use of these commons can lead to the tragedy of the commons. Individuals generate demand for the resource exceeding its supply. That is to say that every individual who consumes an added quantity of the resource prevents other individuals from obtaining it.

(118)　(D) Overgrazing pasturelands.

As a metaphor, Garrett Hardin projected pastureland open to all. He was of the viewpoint that in such common pasturelands, each herder receives an immediate individual benefit from increasing the quantity of livestock to graze on the pasture. In such a system, everyone has access to the pasture with no rules on a sustainable amount of grazing. According to Hardin, the tragedy is that the system compels individuals to increase their herd without any limit. Every individual fight in his/her self-interests is led at the cost of the community interests, causing the exploitation of common-pool natural resources.

(119)　(A) The conflict between individual and collective responsibility.

The tragedy of the commons is based on the inherent tension between individuals and collective interests in the use of a common property. People become more selfish and overly demand for more resources. In such a tragedy, individuals develop an incentive to consume resources at the expense of other individuals' share of those commons. There are no regulations to ensure equal distribution of the resources, causing overconsumption, excessive demand, lower investments, and potential depletion of resources.

(120)    (A) Infancy.

The first 18 months of an individual's life are defined by the nurturing ability of his/her parents. In this stage, the individual develops qualities such as confidence and security. However, the infant might develop qualities such as insecurity and mistrust if he/she is not provided with suitable care and attention.

(121)    (C) Psychosocial.

Erikson's Eight Stages of Development are central to the psychosocial context. According to this theory, social work practice studies the accumulative effect of family, society, and other external factors on an individual's personality. Erik Erikson was of the view that individuals go through eight interrelated stages of development in their lifespan.

(122)    (C) 8.

According to Erik Erikson's views based on the psychosocial theory, individuals had to go through eight interrelated stages of development in their lifespan. These eight stages include: infancy (from birth to 18 months), toddlerhood (from 18 months to 3 years), middle childhood (pre-school age), late childhood (6 to 12 years), adolescence (12 to 18 years), early adulthood, middle adulthood and late adulthood (over 65 years). Erikson was central to the idea that the ability to evolve through these stages effectively is based on biological and sociocultural factors.

(123)    (A) The prototype helps to enable the development of internal processes.

Interpersonal development is central to the idea that an individual's early relations reflect his/her later relations. That is to say that early peer relationships of an individual have a profound influence on the relationships that he/she might have later in life.

(124)   (A) Because if unsuccessful, the individual will develop anxiety and insecurity.

The influence of close family, father, and mother marks the first 18 months of an individual's life. In this stage, the individual develops qualities such as confidence, trust, and security. However, if there is a lack of suitable care and an adequate environment in this phase of growth, the individual might develop qualities such as insecurity and mistrust.

(125)   (D) Life versus death.

Erikson's stages of development involve all factors such as trust versus mistrust, industry versus inferiority, intimacy versus isolation, trust versus mistrust, and autonomy versus shame. However, it does not explain the concept of life versus death.

(126)   (B) Intimacy versus isolation.

The young adulthood phase of Erikson's Stages of Development is concerned with the key trait of intimacy versus isolation. The focus of this stage is on setting up committed relationships with other individuals. Romantic relationships are significant, but friendships and other family relationships also influence this stage of development. Most young adults look to settle down with their families in this phase. However, if unsuccessful in forming satisfying relationships, individuals fall prey to isolation.

(127)   (B) Wisdom.

The central conflict in the late adulthood of Erikson's Stages of Development focuses on integrity versus despair, which involves reflecting on your life. The individuals who are unsuccessful at resolving this conflict will look back with regret. One the other hand, successful individuals will feel a sense of satisfaction and fulfillment with the life they have lived. Erikson was of the viewpoint that those who are successful in this stage develop an understanding of wisdom.

(128)  (B) Ego identity.

Erikson described ego identity as the conscious self that people develop through each stage of development. The ego identity is ever-changing throughout an individual's lifespan. Because these experiences are evolving with each phase of development, individuals face new encounters at each development stage that can either strengthen or weaken their ego identity.

(129)  (B) A preschooler insisting on picking out food and clothes of her own choice.

Autonomy versus shame is a significant psychosocial conflict in the preschool age. This stage of development is central to developing a sense of autonomy, independence, and control. In this stage of development, children develop the desire to copy their adults. Preschoolers are more experimentative with their lives, and it is vital to give children a chance to choose actions on their own even if they make mistakes as it creates a sense of confidence in independence in them.

(130)  (A) There is an unconscious self-realization strength within everyone.

Sigmund Freud's psychoanalytical approach was based on the conscious and unconscious forces in individuals like desires and beliefs. These assumptions are based on psychodynamic theories that explain childhood experience as a strong influence in shaping individuals' personalities.

(131)  (D) Generativity versus stagnation.

Generativity versus stagnation is the conflict in this stage of development. Individuals are faced with responsibilities in this phase and may try to take on more significant roles in society to improve welfare. In this stage, they are fearful of being inactive and unable to do something meaningful with their lives, which may result in major alterations in their lives.

(132)  (C) Defense mechanisms.

The human mind uses the ego's defense mechanisms that are the psychological strategies to ward off the inappropriate id impulses. The ego of an individual functions to meet the fundamental needs and requirements of the id in a socially adequate way. The ego is the modified fragment of the id, according to Sigmund Freud. The external world directly influences the ego, and it works by reason, unlike the id that is irrational and unrealistic.

(133)  (C) Segment of the human psyche that is the storehouse of innate needs.

The id is the part of the psyche that functions at the unconscious level. It is focused on the desires and instincts of an individual. The instincts include the that of survival and death. In short, impulsive instincts and motivations make up the id of the human mind.

(134)  (D) The superego.

In the psychoanalytic approach, the superego denotes the integration of values that are learned from either parents or society. The superego of the human psyche motivates individuals to act in morally acceptable ways. It is because the superego of the human psyche is related to a sense of principles and morality. The superego also controls the impulses of the id, such as sex and aggression. On the contrary, the superego also influences the ego to convert realistic areas of interest to moralistic ones.

(135)  (C) The superego.

According to Sigmund Freud, an infant's brain is all id, and only later are ego and superego developed. Moreover, the superego is the last thing to develop in the human psyche.

(136)  (B) Attainment by all peoples of the highest possible level of health.

The World Health Organization is the world's largest health-related organization to exist currently. Their primary goal relies on coordinating with international health within the United Nations. The constitution had set its objective that depicted WHO's efforts to ensure the well-being of every individual.

(137)   (A) Devise healthcare policies and regulations.

Out of the many objectives the WHO has, one of them aims at formulating policies and regulations that are in the best interests of communities worldwide. These healthcare regulations could be a means of precaution, awareness, or any kind of assistance particularly needed in that domain.

(138)   (D) The quality of life is directly influenced by social, political, and economic events.

Any changes or an occurrence that affects the social, political, or economic values of a country has a direct and significant impact on the quality and rights of human lives, globally.

(139)   (D) Social, political, and economic events.

The beliefs of international social work practice state that human deprivation and any social injustice that may prevail in a state is often a consequence of a disturbance in social, political, and economic events.

(140)   (D) Empathic behavior.

The beliefs of international social work practice stem from problems that arise and are closely linked to social injustice, discrimination, and factors that impact human lives. On the contrary, having empathic behavior towards individuals and underprivileged communities could be a form of a core value or a social worker's goal.

(141)   (A) Eliminating barriers.

Despite the progression of professionalism in social activism, the developments have led to some hindrances, most of which are historical. Still, they tend to disrupt the framework for workers, eliminating barriers deals with oppression and discrimination within communities and minorities.

(142)   (A) Enhancing global development and assisting communities.

International social work aims at consistently improving circumstances to reach enhanced opportunities for global development and growth. It also caters to and supports underprivileged communities that lack fundamental human rights.

(143)   (C) Maintaining a balance between social and economic development.

Having an in-depth understanding of the vitality of a balanced approach in terms of social and economic development is essential to respond to situations where both factors coexist in a vulnerable state. Both are directly related and have an impact on each other. Thus, organizations must find the ideal balance between providing humanitarian aid without exhausting the economy but instead to increase the HDI (Human Development Index), for instance, which would be benefitting.

(144)   (B) Having faith in peace.

As a means of social work practice, development can be most effective with the existence of global peace; therefore, faith in peace remains distinct from the goals of international social work. Social work is more committed to delivering community support alongside enhancing global development.

(145)   (D) It helps the client view the problem from a different perspective as a separate entity.

Personifying problems in narrative therapy allows social workers to enlighten clients with the fact of how their problems do not define them as a person, and using this technique, the client can look at the problem as an entity that is not directly related to himself. It helps the client and worker to address the problem collectively.

(146)   (A) Seven-stage crisis.

The seven-stage crisis is a crisis intervention technique that involves the client and worker to go through various steps to counter the issue rather than overlooking the problem itself as practiced in solution-based therapy.

(147)   (A) Concise.

The task-centered practice is a model that emphasizes the client reaching milestones with the objectives that are set to be achieved. In a brief span of eight-ten sessions, this model is used over several individuals, groups, and families and allows a worker to identify the client's preferences and strengths.

(148)   (B) It depends on the ability of the worker.

Though TCP may have separate phases that are quite distinct from one another, it is not rare for these phases to overlap, causing confusion that disrupts the framework of this process. However, it has been argued that workers who possess enough experience and knowledge to tackle such situations could get through by maximizing the benefit from every phase.

(149)   (A) Diversification of cultural values and lives.

Social discrimination and disregard for minorities and communities with differences, deteriorate the environmental conditions of a country, and have a direct impact on the quality of human lives. The understanding of cultural values for protection and developmental purposes is essential.

(150)   (D) Assistance to counter any global issues that may arise as a result of crises that affect humanity.

IFRC collaborates with partners over the mezzo and macro level in an attempt to improve economic, social, and political conditions. The initiatives taken by these alliances aid the welfare-orientated organizations, such as IFRC, to collectively tackle any global humanitarian challenges that may arise on a large scale.